Man, Husband, Father

by
Buddy Harrison

Harrison House
Tulsa, Oklahoma

Man, Husband, Father
ISBN 0-89274-792-7
Copyright © 1995 by Buddy Harrison
P. O. Box 35443
Tulsa, Oklahoma 74153

Published by Harrison House, Inc.
P. O. Box 35035
Tulsa, Oklahoma 74153

Contents

Prologue

It is 11 p.m. at the local supermarket. A tall, thin gentleman walks with a shuffle older than his 41 years, and tired eyes look out from under an expensive Stetson. He has been wandering the aisles of the supermarket for over an hour and has only three items in his cart: a bottle of scotch he knows he will put back because he is smart enough to realize there are no real answers there; a loaf of extra sour sourdough French bread, just because he likes it; and the latest Louis L'Amour western. Perhaps he can lose himself in another time; a time when what it takes to be a man is clear and plain.

Only yesterday he had told his psychiatrist he felt people didn't really see him when they looked at him. At 41 years of age and the head of his own financial services company, he had achieved a level of success many would have envied, and did. But the truth was, he was frustrated and quite dissatisfied with his life. No, make that with himself.

Then, somewhere between the hamburger buns and the lunch meat counter, he was startled by a realization that would change his life. In the middle of hunting for a decent barbecue sauce, it occurred to him: he was not a man in his own eyes!

How could this be? He was of full stature, healthy and virile. Back in his office downtown he had an "ego wall" full of awards, citations and civic proclamations; there was even a letter of appreciation from the President of the United States. His Lexus was parked nightly in the garage of one of the nicest homes in the suburbs, and he golfed regularly with the most prominent businessmen in town.

7

On the home front, his marriage of 11 years, (his second), was perking along OK. It was not the sparkling dream he had hoped it would be, but then neither were any of his friends' marriages. He guessed that was just the way it was. Things got flat after awhile. His children were about average for their age but, here again, he was guessing. His priorities did not really include them much, except on weekends, but then, after all, he was engaged in a challenging climb up the ladder of business success.

Now, perched high atop that ladder and becoming increasingly dissatisfied, he began to feel the weight of the price he had paid pulling him down like rocks in a backpack. Each step up was harder than the last. Even as his frustration mounted, his will, his drive and his energy were all deserting him. Success was not supposed to cost you your manhood, he thought, it was supposed to confirm it. But he didn't feel confirmed, he felt hollow.

As he steered the shopping cart toward the registers he passed the liquor section. He put the scotch back, as he knew he would. Register five was the only one open at this hour and, as he entered the lane, the aproned young man had just finished wiping off the scanner for the fifth time. It had been a slow night. The young man's name tag called him Arthur.

The gentleman placed his purchases on the moving belt. Beep! A dollar seventy-nine for the sourdough bread. Beep! Four ninety-five for the novel. The gentleman handed Arthur a ten and received his change.

"Thanks," the gentleman muttered, looking once again at the young man's name tag, "Arthur."

"You're welcome, Sir," the checker drawled. "Have a good evening." He flashed a sincere smile.

When the gentleman took his limp sack of groceries from Arthur's hand, he noticed something curious. Pinned to the young man's shirt sleeve, right above a tattoo on his forearm, was a button which read, "Admit it, you need Jesus."

"Isn't that just a bit confusing there, Arthur?" the gentleman asked, alternately pointing to the tattoo and the pin. He almost managed to disguise the cynicism in his voice.

Arthur broke into a big grin and laughed easily. "No sir, not to me," he said, "I got that tattoo trying to prove to myself I was a man. Didn't work, though. All I really needed was Jesus."

Arthur's face was radiant. He really did have something, this young man, and for the briefest moment, the gentleman searched his face for the answers he so desperately needed. Unable to think of anything else to say, he simply nodded. Then lowering his head, he turned and left the store.

Two blocks away everything suddenly made sense. He realized what had been eluding him. It was too simple, but he should have known. It was true, he admitted. He too needed Jesus.

* * *

Three months later you would not have known the man. Everything wasn't perfect by a long stretch, but his confidence and self-satisfaction were readily apparent. Now, beyond any question, he knew he was a man. His family had even noticed the dramatic change.

What had happened? Now his manhood was being defined and confirmed not by his accomplishments, but by a relationship. He had chosen to travel an adventurous path the Lord Jesus invites all His men to walk: the path to becoming fulfilled by being conformed to *His* image of man, husband and father.

9

This book is a sort of trail map to guide you to manhood in Christ Jesus. It is written to help you discern the Kingdom's mile markers along the way, and to help you mark your progress on the path ahead of you. Enjoy the trail. It is a real adventure!

1
Now You're A Man!
My Early Years

As a kid growing up in East Texas I longed for the day when I would be called a man! Most of all, I wanted to hear my father call me that. You see, in Texas manhood was a badge of respect worn with great honor, and an achievement second to none. The ethics of the Old West still spoke into the lives of every young boy stretching for manhood. Like most young men I wanted to know my father was proud of me, and that I pleased him. I longed for the day he would acknowledge that I had arrived.

In high school I had two loves, football and a pretty little gal I planned to marry. By the time graduation came around I had been offered three different football scholarships. So here I was trying to decide which college to attend and at the same time trying to plan a way to ask the girl I was crazy about to marry me.

Two things happened right about then which dramatically changed the course of my life. I lost one love and gained another, and in the middle of it all, my dad called me a man. Oddly enough, everything happened on the same night.

Let me back up here for a minute and fill you in. At that time, spiritual things had very little place in my life. The only reason I went to church was out of respect for my mother. My grandfather had imparted faith to me as a very young boy, but I had grown far away from God for various

11

reasons...one of them being the lifestyle of my father, a professional gambler.

And the church I was attending at the time was no help. I'll never forget going to a Sunday School class one morning as a young teenager. The fact that I loved football was already known around town, and I had already acquired a considerable reputation for my playing skill. Shortly after I walked into the class, the teacher recognized who I was, pointed her finger at me and said, "You will go to hell for playing football."

I abruptly told her where *she* could go and walked out. I went and got Mama and we left right then. "I love you," I told her, "but we aren't coming back here!"

Six months later Mama asked me to go with her to another church, this time, in a nearby town. The pastor's daughter was in my class, and what I didn't know was she had told her father all about me. The second Sunday we visited, we walked into church while Pastor was making announcements. Suddenly he stopped, looked straight at me and asked, "Did we win the football game Friday night?" I couldn't believe it!

Remember, one of my goals at this point was to have my manliness confirmed, and here was a pastor affirming football, and me for playing it, all at the same time. I was hooked! Maybe there was something to this church stuff after all.

Night of Nights

Shortly after I had graduated I was on my way to pick up my girlfriend one evening for what was to be a very important night. On the way to her house I drove by a church, and I remember thinking as I passed it, I should take her to church sometime.

That night I waited around until 2 a.m. for her to come home. She never showed up. (I found out later she had stood me up for a date with another guy!)

I finally left in a fit of anger! I had never been angrier in my young life than I was at that moment. On the way home I passed that same church again, and this time I stopped. *God and I were going to have it out!* You see, I thought God was in church at the altar, and the only way to reach Him was for me to meet Him there. I didn't know I could meet Him on the street, in my car, anywhere.

The church double doors were locked, but I kicked them in anyway. Fumbling in the near total darkness, I attempted to work my way down to the altar at the front. I was angry, hurt, depressed, and needed God desperately. As I stumbled over and crashed into things in the darkened church, I cried out, "Dear God, God of my grandfather, I need to get saved...I need help. You're down there and I'm back up here. If I keep going like this, I'll fall and break my neck, die and go to hell before I ever have a chance to get there."

About that time a light shone at my feet. It was like a spotlight. Nobody instructed me, but I suddenly had a desire to step into it. When I did, it moved and I just followed that light all the way to the altar. God met me where I was and moved supernaturally to get me to the altar where I could make everything right. It was a glorious experience! I cried, I prayed, I shouted, I rejoiced.

While I was there, I suddenly remembered hearing my mama's prayers for me one night, a while back, when I was still running from God.

I had been trying to get home before my Dad one night...he usually got in between 3 and 5 a.m., but I was running real late. Thinking he was already home, I tried to sneak into the house. When I got inside I heard Mama praying, "Lord, bring my husband home safe: Lord, bring my son home safe. Don't let anything evil come to them, keep Your hand upon them, bring them home safe."

I got so intrigued listening to Mama pray I walked right into something and it crashed to the floor. Mama slipped into bed and acted like she was asleep. But after I got into bed I heard her slip quietly to the floor, onto her knees, and say, "Father, thank You for bringing my son home safe. Now Father, bring my husband home safe."

That night, in a darkened church, praying at the altar, I thought of Mama's prayers. Right then I wanted nothing more in the whole world than to have her pray with me. I went home, got her out of bed and we both went down to that church. We laughed and shouted and cried and prayed, danced all over the front of that church until 5 o'clock in the morning!

We returned home just before Dad walked in. Mama made him something to eat and when she began to serve him, I started talking. It fairly jumped out. "I found God tonight and I want to go to a Christian school to be around other Christians." I braced myself, expecting him to make fun of me, as he had done so often. He looked at me with a strange, almost distant look on his face and tears came into his eyes. He spoke after a moment and when he did his voice broke. "Son, I'm proud of you...you're a man!"

What glorious words those were to my ears. It was the first time I can ever remember realizing I had pleased my father. He was actually proud of me and what was more, he had said so. He had called me a man!

In one night I had gotten saved and had my father fulfill one of my deepest longings for his approval. I remember thinking, it just could not get any better than this. I was wrong. It got better the more I learned about what all had actually happened to me that night.

Just as the Lord did for me, He can do for you, too, my brother. I would like this book to shine a light on your path to help you navigate through the obstacles in your life. It is my privilege to speak into your life by this book. I hope it will help you become everything the Lord intended you to be as a man, a husband, and a father.

2
Super Man, Spirit Man

When I was a boy, my hero was Superman. I often pretended to be like him. Imagining I was Clark Kent, I would get Mama's longest towel, shake it out real good, flip it back around and tie it under my neck. Then I would get up on top of something, usually the chest of drawers, make sure my cape was ready, hold up my arms, and loudly proclaim, "Da dum da dum da dum...here I am, faster than a speeding bullet, more powerful than a locomotive, able to leap tall buildings in a single bound." I was all primed for the moment, up, up and away! At least, I thought so! But soon it was down, down in dismay! I still have a scar today to prove it!

It is one thing to play like Superman, and another thing to be him. When it finally dawned on me I would never really *be* Superman, I realized I would have to settle for being just a mere man. But then I discovered God's plan, and found out I could be much more than just a mere man. God had a not-so-secret identity for me.

When Jesus calmed the stormy seas, His disciples exclaimed, **What manner of man is this!** (Luke 8:25). Jesus had told them to go across the lake, but the nasty weather conditions caused fear to rise up in them and they forgot His words. Often in our own situations, even when we have heard the Word, stormy circumstances arise. When that happens we can unwittingly enter the danger zone. And the danger is we might allow our faith to be overcome by fear. We can forget what manner of men we really are. If we allow that to occur, then we *are* mere men.

Jesus knew who He was! He knew and operated in His authority and realized His supernatural abilities. A storm was not about to keep Him from accomplishing His goals. He was a SUPERNATURAL MAN and He knew it. What about us? Are we destined to be just mere men? Is there a new identity for us? Let us examine what God's Word says about us. Second Corinthians 5:17 says, **Therefore if any man be in Christ, he is a new creature: old things are passed away; behold, all things are become new.**

New "creatures" — did you know that another way of saying **new creature** would be "a brand new species"? We are no longer mere men, but supernatural men, exactly like Jesus. We got that way by being born again of a supernatural God. Being born again by the Spirit of God puts us in a different dimension, a new level, a league by ourselves. We truly have a new identity.

A New Family

Interestingly enough, not only are we new creatures, born of supernatural blood but, like any new creature, we have a new family. We are now children of God. His life resides in us. He is our Father, and we are His sons! Ephesians 1:5, **Having predestinated us unto the adoption of children by Jesus Christ to himself, according to the good pleasure of his will.**

Carrying this out a bit further, we can also understand that, just like in the natural realm, certain natural traits are transferred to children by birth. So too, in the supernatural realm. The similarities are often obvious.

When my son was still young, others commented on how much he was like me. He was always looking for a good deal, and he knew how to make money! One time we had bought a half case of grapefruits and stored them in the garage. Well, we traveled so much that we never did eat them all and they began to harden and turn brown in the garage. Our son, Damon, discovered them and figured he could make some money off those old things. He took them around to the neighbors and actually sold those hardened, brown grapefruits. Our neighbors, believe it or not, paid good hard money for them!

Like Father, Like Son

People were always saying to Damon, "Like father, like son!" Well, the devil used that same phrase to torment me for years because I struggled with some of the same negative traits my father had. I would hear, "Like father, like son...you're just like him, and you always will be." I would get so irritated and yet, by all appearances, I was headed that way. I kept falling into the same old traps, making the same mistakes I had seen my father make. I was nearly convinced I would always be that way because I was just like him. I became depressed and desperate.

Then one day God spoke up on the inside of me and said, "That's right, Son, like Father, like son. I'm your Father, and you're My son!" That set me free because I realized my spiritual Father's character far outweighed the natural traits that had been dominating me. I was born again of my heavenly Father, with His attributes, His abilities, His nature in me. No longer was I mere man, but a supernatural man! A supernatural man able to operate in two dimensions at the same time. He had created me to be victorious in both.

The powers Superman had could not even compare to the supernatural arsenal with which my heavenly Father had equipped me.

A speeding bullet was slow compared to how fast I was able to move into the throne room of God and stand in His very presence to make my requests known.

A locomotive's power was puny compared to the power in the name of Jesus, which I had full authority to use.

; over tall buildings was child's play compared
.e to move not only in the natural dimension, but
rnatural dimension as well. In that dimension I
could pull down strongholds that dwarf the tallest
buildings.

But, just like Superman had to learn how to use his
super powers, we have to learn how to develop in spiritual
things. How do we do that? Ephesians 5:1, **Be ye therefore
followers of God, as dear children....** One translation, ASV,
says we are to **be imitators of God, as beloved children**.

That is what children do — they walk around imitating
their parents. They walk like them, talk like them, think like
them. Now if a child never lives in his parents'
environment, never has fellowship with them, then those
things don't always rub off on him, nor does he pick up
certain traits. But if the child is with his parents at all, he
will pick up some characteristics especially in the early,
more influential years of development.

We are the same way with God — if we spend time with
Him, His ways are going to affect us. The different aspects,
characteristics of God the Father, Jesus the Son, and the
Holy Spirit will rub off on us. Some traits we are born with
when we are born again, but some only come through
fellowship with the Godhead. Each Person of the Trinity
has traits we need and should desire.

The main characteristic of the Father is love. The nature
of Jesus is to be the reconciler of man to God, and, of man to
his fellowmen, and the nature of the Holy Spirit, Who lives
on the inside of us, is that of a revelator, teacher, and helper.
We need the teaching ministry of the Holy Spirit on a daily
basis to grow in spiritual things.

As we develop relationship with all three persons of the
Godhead, we will take on their characteristics. We will walk
in love with all men. We will become agents of reconciliation

for those who are lost, and we will be able to receive and operate in the revelation of the Holy Spirit.

Benefits Of Relationship

Relationship brings certain benefits in natural families as well as in our spiritual family. But some benefits come just because we are in fellowship with one another. If my children stopped talking to me, quit having anything to do with me, there would be some blessings they would never enjoy. Many times we cut ourselves off from the blessings of God in the same way.

I remember one time when my daughter Candy and I were out running errands together. We stopped on the way home to get a milkshake. Candy was finishing her shake when she walked into the house. My son, Damon, saw it and yelled, "That's not fair, Dad, why didn't I get a shake?" We did not deliberately leave him out, but he simply was not with us at the time. So that is all I said to him, "Son, you weren't with us." Certain blessings can only come from fellowshipping!

Even in ministry, while the anointing is transferable, much of its development comes through fellowship. My own life is a good example. Kenneth Hagin is both my father-in-law and a spiritual father to me. I worked for several years in his ministry before going out on my own. Even after I left his employ, it used to frustrate me that I had become so much like him because I wanted very much to be myself, to have a ministry that was just me.

But you cannot spend ten years with a great man of God like Kenneth Hagin without some of it rubbing off on you. I would catch myself making certain gestures just like him, even talking like him. Others noticed it. People even introduced me by his name at times. When you love somebody and spend time with them, it becomes an unconscious thing to be like them.

So it is with your heavenly Father. Until you spend time in your heavenly Father's presence, the fullness of His attributes and blessings won't be in your life. You won't walk as He walks, talk as He talks, see things as He does, nor enjoy all of His benefits. So instead of asking why others are getting blessed when you are not, spend time with Him, loving and enjoying His presence!

Joint-Heirs With Jesus

Not only are we children of God, but according to Romans 8:17, **And if children, then heirs; heirs of God, and joint-heirs with Christ....** Joint means equal entitlement. We have equal inheritance with our Brother Jesus Christ. That means everything He has is ours to share. He has given us all His authority, the power of attorney to use His name, which is above every name, and told us to go do the works He did. In fact, He even told us we would do greater works than He did. He wants us to have even more than He had here on earth.

Not only are we new creatures in Christ, children of God, with His supernatural nature and attributes, and joint-heirs with Jesus, but He also made us righteous. **For he hath made him to be sin for us, who knew no sin; that we might be made the righteousness of God in him** (2 Cor. 5:21). Now think about this — *He's made us His righteousness.* Do you really understand what that means? Not only is our sin not held against us, but God keeps no record of it.

Righteousness means to be able to come into God's presence without any sense of sin, condemnation, guilt or inferiority! So anytime we have an awareness of those things, we need to confess any sin, for **...he is faithful and just to forgive us our sins, and to cleanse us from all unrighteousness** (1 John 1:9). He chooses to remember them no more and says, "Come on in, son, you belong with me." He never mentions that sin again to us, for we are cleansed with the blood of Jesus.

Now it is for sure that the devil remembers our sins and does not want us to forget them. One of his strategies is to taunt us with those memories, condemn us, and tell us we are just scum. Well, that is a lie — we are righteous, not because of us, but because of Jesus, whose death made us that way when we accepted Him as Lord and Savior. But if we listen to the devil, instead of God, we will forget who we are — no longer mere men, but God's supernatural men.

In God's eyes we are clothed in robes of righteousness which are white and spotless. I may not look righteous, but I am, because the Word says so. I may not look like Superman, but just like Clark Kent, I go in and shuck off those old clothes, slip into my robe of righteousness and go "up, up and away" into victory with God.

Superman was said to be more powerful than a locomotive, but when we do the works of Jesus and use His name, we walk in great dynamic power — dynamite kind of power. In addition, Revelation 5:10 says, **And hast made us unto our God kings and priests: and we shall reign on the earth.** Kings have power, they rule kingdoms and when they speak, when they decree a thing, when they make a command, it is carried out! Ecclesiastes says, **Where the word of a king is, there is power** (8:4). When we speak the word of God, in the authority given to us, power is released! More power than any locomotive!

Not only am I a new creature, a child of God, a joint-heir with Jesus Christ, the righteousness of God, a King who rules and reigns in life, but I am also a priest. I can come boldly to the throne of God, without hesitation, without reservation, without any reluctance whatsoever. He is my Father, I am His child; I belong there! Unlike Clark Kent, who disguised his true identity, I can proudly proclaim who I am! It is all in the Word, written and established forever, and I simply need to believe it and walk in it! God's SUPERNATURAL MAN, that's me!

Now, even Superman had needs, but I can boldly make my requests known because all I need has already been provided through Jesus. First Corinthians 1:30 says, **But of him are ye in Christ Jesus, who of God is made unto us wisdom, and righteousness, and sanctification, and redemption....** He has provided everything essential to godliness, redeemed me from poverty, sickness, and sin, made me everything I ever dreamed of being. The Superman I idolized as a kid was simply the creation of some clever comic strip writers, but I am the creation of the Almighty God. I no longer have to pretend to be somebody great. Like Paul, **...by the grace of God I am what I am....** (2 Cor. 15:10). And what I am in Christ is far beyond anything I ever dreamt about as a boy.

The Key To Spiritual Power

But be ye doers of the word and not hearers only, deceiving your own selves. For if any be a hearer of the word, and not a doer, he is like unto a man beholding his natural face in a glass: for he beholdeth himself, and goeth his way, and straightway forgetteth what manner of man he was.

James 1:22-24

The Word of God is like a mirror, reflecting us as we truly are. Now it is up to us to receive it and believe it. If we do not, we deceive ourselves. When Clark Kent looked in his mirror, he only saw a mere man staring back at him. It was not until he put on his Superman garments that he changed into the image of the man he could be. When we look in our natural mirrors we may only see ourselves as mere men, but the mirror of God's Word shows us differently. Therefore, it is not a matter of hiding in a telephone booth or closet and changing into some red, gold and blue outfit and cape — it is a matter of seeing ourselves in God's mirror as He does, and walking in it! You *really are* God's SUPERNATURAL MAN, and don't forget it!

It is important that you catch an accurate vision of what God did in birthing you by His Spirit into the new creation you now are! Once you grasp the true significance of what the Lord has done for you, there will be no holding you back!

3
Watch Where You're Walking!

Becoming a Super Man takes no effort on our part — Jesus already accomplished it for us. Endeavoring to live the godly life, however, does take some effort on our part. SUPERNATURAL MAN is *who* we are, but walking in the godly lifestyle is *what we do* with who we are!

God laid out the plan for how to walk that godly lifestyle for us in Psalm 1:1-3:

> **Blessed is the man that walketh not in the counsel of the ungodly, nor standeth in the way of sinners, nor sitteth in the seat of the scornful. But his delight is in the law of the Lord; and in his law doth he meditate day and night. And he shall be like a tree planted by the rivers of water, that bringeth forth his fruit in his season; his leaf also shall not wither; and whatsoever he doeth shall prosper.**

Notice this Psalm speaks of progression. First, the man walks, then he stands and finally, he sits a spell. It all starts with where he walks! When it comes to the things of God, our walk is not only vitally important but each step along the way is significant.

Psalm 37:23: **The steps of a good man are ordered of the Lord; and he delighteth in his way.**

Have you considered where you are walking? Are you on God's path? Is He ordering your steps?

You may not realize it, but you are always walking in someone's counsel. The question is, is it God's counsel or man's? The Psalmist declared the man who walks *not* in ungodly counsel is blessed.

The Hebrew definition for the word *counsel*[1] in Psalm 1 is "to set or lay a foundation." Foundations are laid or set with a particular structure in mind. They are built to specific standards in order to securely withstand the elements and uphold the structures which are built upon them. Usually, foundations are unseen, but they are vitally important to the overall structure. They are laid to support a certain design or a particular structure and no other kind.

The first verse in Psalm 1 is saying a man is blessed according to the foundation he walks upon. When I walk in a hotel room on the fiftieth floor I certainly hope the foundation of that building is strong and secure, yet I rarely think about it. If that floor were to begin shaking as I walked across it, and the windows began rattling, I would question the wisdom of staying in that room. In fact, I would get out of there real quick!

It works the same way in our lives. When things are shaking us or we get rattled by circumstances and our lives are not being blessed, something is wrong with our walk. Most likely it is the foundation we are walking on that is unstable.

Back on the Path

One of my staff tells the story about a period he and his wife went through where nothing they did would bring them out of the financial hole they were in. They studied books on finances. They fasted and prayed. They asked for advice. Nothing worked. Finally, one night as they were sharing the day's events with each other it dawned on them that neither one of them had mentioned spending any time in the Word recently. They had become so preoccupied with solving their problem they had neglected their foundational time with the Lord in His Word.

Once they resumed their former schedule, trusting the Lord to supply, it wasn't but just a few days and Word of the Lord came to them as to what they should do. He had been aware of their situation all the time, but His counsel comes out of relationship with Him, not preoccupation with our problems.

Proverbs 8:14 states, **Counsel is mine, and sound wisdom: I am understanding; I have strength.** Godly counsel will hold up under any conditions, regardless of what else is going on. Building upon God's counsel brings security and safety.

Jesus was called Wonderful, Counsellor by the prophet Isaiah (9:16). Jesus and the Word are One, according to John 1:14. Jesus is also referred to as our advocate or lawyer (1 John 2:1). As in a court of law, when a person gives his testimony he is giving his solemn word; so too, God's testimonies are His Word. Psalm 119:24 tells us: **Thy testimonies also are my delight and my counsellors.** Therefore, our first and foremost source of counsel should be the Word of God, written under the inspiration of the Holy Spirit.

Heeding God's Counsel

Before David slew Goliath (1 Sam. 1:7) several people tried to counsel him otherwise. His brothers mocked him, reminding him that he was simply a shepherd. They accused him of wrong motives. The Israelites ridiculed him. King Saul told David he was too young, and then, when he couldn't change the lad's mind, tried to persuade him to wear his armor which was much too large. But David didn't take their counsel. His foundation had been laid already; his steps were ordered of the Lord. He walked away from their advice, and took counsel instead from the testimonies of God's Word. Then he rehearsed his past victories, his own testimonies of how God had worked in his life. We know the outcome, how David killed the giant with one stone and a slingshot. He became a blessed man, because he walked on a firm foundation of God's Word and in godly counsel.

I thank God for the godly men who have given me wise counsel over the years. Because Kenneth Hagin has been a spiritual father to me, I often seek his advice. Proverbs 20:5 states, **Counsel in the heart of man is like deep water; but a man of understanding will draw it out.** Brother Hagin is a man of few words, yet there is such wisdom within him. Sometimes it takes effort on my part to draw it out, but what restoration and refreshing he has brought to my heart through his godly counsel.

Ignoring godly counsel and trying to live by your own wisdom can have disastrous consequences. At one time in my life, while I was running from God, I flagrantly insulted Brother Hagin, even blew cigar smoke in his face. I taunted Sister Hagin unmercifully. But they never returned the evil towards me; they always accepted me even at my worst. How I appreciate and thank God for their influence in my life.

God has also provided me with an advisory board and people in leadership to assist me in the policy making decisions that an international ministry like Faith Christian Fellowship requires. I also have my pastor of the home church in Tulsa to rely upon for counsel when needed! He is a great comfort to my heart and a tremendous asset to me. I am a blessed man because of these men and women who supply me with godly counsel.

The Most Important Counsel, Husband

But, perhaps the most important and sometimes overlooked counsel a man has is that of a godly wife. My wife Pat is full of wisdom because she is also full of God's Word and His Holy Spirit. And like God told Abraham concerning listening to his wife (Gen. 21:12), there are times

I need to listen to mine! In fact, many times she has given me counsel right from the heart of God.

I will never forget the time I was struggling with a particular issue, one which had brought much heartache to my family. I had been delivered from demonic activity, but was questioning that deliverance because of a recent setback. Therefore, I lived in guilt and condemnation on a daily basis instead of taking a stand against the enemy. I was feeling so guilty about what I had done, and the pain I had brought to those who meant so much to me, when Pat spoke up. She reminded me that familiar spirits once operated in my life to a great degree. She observed how those same spirits, working through others, attempted to pull me back into repeating those old patterns.

What a relief Pat's insights were to my heart. And how precious she was to share those truths with me even though my actions had caused her much grief. Yes, it pays to have a good wife, one who **...will do him good and not evil all the days of her life** (Prov. 31:13).

Observing where you walk is important because sooner or later you will stop and stand wherever you are walking. Proverbs 7:8 illustrates this clearly in speaking of a young man.

Passing through the street near her corner; and he went the way to her house, in the twilight, in the evening, in the black and dark night; And, behold, there met him a woman with the attire of an harlot, and subtle of heart.

That young man's first mistake was where he walked — near her house. Pretty soon, he stood there, long enough for the woman to allure him. That passage goes on to describe how she enticed him with flattering speech and how easily he succumbed to her invitation. Later he may have wondered how it all happened. He simply walked there, then he stood there! Then he fell into her trap.

Armed And Ready

Where are you standing in your walk? Ephesians 6:13-18 tells us how to stand!

Wherefore take unto you the whole armour of God, that ye may be able to with*stand* in the evil day, and having done all, to *stand*.

***Stand* therefore, having your loins girt about with truth, and having on the breastplate of righteousness; and your feet shod with the preparation of the gospel of peace;**

Above all, taking the shield of faith, wherewith ye shall be able to quench all the fiery darts of the wicked. And take the helmet of salvation, and the sword of the Spirit, which is the Word of God:

Praying always with all prayer and supplication in the Spirit....

Did you notice it says to stand three different times in that passage? Then it shows us how to stand, *entirely clothed* in God's armour. Unlike Saul's armour, God's armour will always fit. But we must wear it for it to do us any good. In addition, we are to be praying *always* in the Spirit. Always! That does not leave any time out, does it?

No matter where you are walking, pray in the Spirit — in your heavenly language. No matter what time of the day or night, pray in the Spirit. Always! I like to think of it as *all ways*, too. In all your ways, pray in the Spirit. **In all thy ways acknowledge him, and he shall direct thy paths** (Prov. 3:5). When I am praying in the Spirit as I walk along, he will direct me, instructing me when to turn, when to take a different path, when to side-step certain hindrances put in my path. He will show me how to walk up hills and through valleys, when to speak to that mountain ahead, and which fig tree to curse. When to stand, when to pursue, when to rest and when to walk on through!

Several years ago when I was pastoring FCF, Tulsa, the Holy Spirit led me to purchase a larger building. I was very frustrated because I just could not seem to find the right building, and I was also more than tired of having to turn people away from our overcrowded Sunday morning services. I cried out to God for help. We had no finances and I had no idea how we could even make the move. The Spirit of God spoke to me, saying, "First, you have to leave where you're at!" Well, that makes sense, you can't go somewhere unless you leave your present place! The next service I announced to my congregation that we would be moving within a certain period of time. In faith, I gave notice to our landlords. Then I heard about a vacant department store on the north side which was for sale.

As I walked through that old store, my mind was racing. My spirit was inspired, and I was praying in the Spirit. The more I walked around that huge building, the more I prayed until I finally knew this was the place. It certainly did not look like a church right then, but I began to see it as a church in the spirit realm. We had no money, but God came through supernaturally. Within days after we had taken occupancy of the building, we had totally remodeled the inside and held our first church service. What a glorious day that was! Why? Because godly counsel came to me as I walked, as I stood, and as I prayed in the Spirit.

Counselors By the Dozen

First Corinthians 14:10 states, **There are, it may be, so many kinds of voices in the world, and none of them is without signification.** You hear voices every day which can influence you. They all have some significance. Since faith comes by hearing, and hearing by the Word of God, then what you hear, the voices you really listen to, will have tremendous impact on your life, and on your decision making.

Many people heard negative voices when they were younger. You may have heard, "You'll never amount to anything," or "You're too dumb," or "You were born poor and you'll die poor." Unless you have renewed your mind to the Word of God, those words are still counseling you, because your foundation was laid upon them.

I know that was the case in my life. It took me years to pull up some perverted foundations I had been taught by some relatives. They were well set, like firm cement with reinforcing wires. They had significance! They even had truth, but not God's truth! They counseled me, guided me, but not in the paths of righteousness!

As you walk down certain paths, and stand in particular places, sooner or later, you are bound to sit down and rest. If you have walked in the counsel of the ungodly, and stood in the way of sinners, then you will soon find yourself sitting with the scornful, as it says in Psalm 1:3.

Have you ever noticed how scornful people mock God and His truths? They are judgmental, self-righteous, bitter and hateful people. They ridicule others, attempting to elevate themselves in the process. Often they themselves have been abused, victims of someone else's hatred.

Sitting with the scornful is like sitting with the devil, yet some folks do it deliberately. They would rather have sympathy than salvation.

When we sit down we usually try to make ourselves comfortable. Our seat becomes a resting place where we position ourselves. Pretty soon the surroundings begin to affect us, but it happens so subtly we rarely notice it. Face it, the devil isn't going to announce his arrival on the scene. But, then again, you wouldn't have taken a seat there unless you had walked there first. And you wouldn't have seated yourself unless you had stood there first, if only for a moment!

We already have a place to sit. According to Ephesians 2:6, **God...raised us up together, and made us sit together**

in heavenly places in Christ Jesus.... That is a positional seat, but are you sitting there on a regular basis? Is it your favorite chair, are you comfortable there? Spiritually, we are seated together with Jesus in that heavenly seat — can you see Him from where you are sitting, where you rest yourself? It is a known fact that our surroundings affect us. How are your surroundings affecting you? These are hard questions for some people reading this, but if you want to be God's man for your family then you will have to deal with your responses, or lack of response, to them.

Jesus said, **If you've seen me, you've seen the Father** (John 14:9). That was not an egotistical statement, but truth! If we are seated with Him in heavenly places, and He lives in and through us, should not others see the Father when they see us? Would your friends, family, fellow employees say they see Jesus, and the Father in your life?

The First Steps

A man needs to repent for walking in the counsel of the ungodly. No, it may not have seemed evil at the time, but the consequences speak for themselves. You may have stumbled in darkness for years in certain areas because of pride and erroneous judgment regarding the paths you have chosen. The Spirit of God would have led you in another way if you had heeded His voice, if you had put away man's reasoning, man's thoughts, and man's opinions. But I have good news for you: it is not too late to change your paths and walk in God's ways. Here is how.

Psalm 1 admonishes us to take delight in the law (the Word) of the Lord, to meditate on it day and night. The word *delight* means "to desire strongly."[2] The primary meaning of the word implies entire inclination towards an object or person. It means to be yielded, pliable, to be bent towards. You may think you cannot do this, but all the power you need is given in God's commands. It is simply ours for the asking, but we must submit ourselves to His will, His Word.

Meditating on His Word day and night helps us yield. We begin to see His character, His continual love and patience with us. Each time we think of His goodness, it is a little easier to "bend" His way.

Have you ever seen a tree that has been shaped in a certain fashion? It took patience on that gardener's part to get that tree to bend properly. It wanted to grow its own way, but soon, with the right trimming and gentle yet firm directing, that tree took on a new design. It is the same way with us. Each day as we meditate on God's Word, little by little, we bend more and more into His perfect fashion. Romans 8:29 tells us that we are predestined **to be conformed to His image.**

I have written a book called, *Just Do It!* which can be of great help to you in this area. It is important to recognize that what you say is what you see and what you see is what you will eventually do! Meditation on God's Word is your key to success in any area of your life. God told Joshua to meditate both day and night and look what he accomplished! (Josh. 1:8.)

Meditating is not difficult, nor is it only a far-Eastern tradition. It involves three facets. First, it means to speak the Word out loud. Second, mutter it to yourself. Third, imagine yourself in the verse. Your faith rises as you hear yourself say the verse over and over. Next, as you mutter it to yourself, chewing it over and over as a cow chews its cud, it becomes digested into your spirit man. Then through the eyes of faith, you begin to "see" it, to imagine yourself with the promise, the truth, the principle.

The Psalmist admonishes us to delight in the Word and meditate on it day and night with the greatest of results — fruitfulness, life and prosperity. I have found in my own life it is impossible for me to maintain a godly lifestyle without some daily time of study and meditating the Word. I spend time dwelling on His truths which pull down mental strongholds from the past. Then when I walk, His Word truly is **a lamp unto my feet, and a light unto my path** (Ps. 119:105). I can see where I am walking, where to stand and where to sit!

What we've been talking about is developing godliness in our character. But remember what your grandmother or mother used to say was next to godliness? Read on.

4
Take Your Bath, Son!

Like the majority of red-blooded American boys, I
didn't much hanker to bath nights! In my estimation, baths
were a waste of good water, time and energy. I never could
figure out why Mama insisted I take them regularly. After
all, I was bound to get dirty all over again the next day! It
wasn't until I became a teenager, interested in the opposite
sex, that I realized the benefits of cleanliness. I discovered
unless I smelled and looked good, I was unwelcome in
certain places. I was downright amazed at the difference it
made. After a while I became so accustomed to being clean,
that I no longer felt comfortable remaining dirty.

In our Christian walk, it is much the same, only instead
of Mama beckoning me to take a bath, it is the Holy Spirit
Who stirs our hearts, showing us in the Word specific areas
of our lives which need cleaning up. But He doesn't just
spotlight the sin, He illuminates the way out of sin! (We'll
talk more about this later).

Dirty Diapers And All

My dad used to say something I have never forgotten.
He would say, "You're my son and I take full responsibility
for that. No matter what you do, you're still my son. Even if
you mess your britches, you're my son. Messy britches and
all, I'll clean up the mess because you belong to me!" These
words may not sound like music to your ears, but when I
had messed up in life, they brought a certain degree of
comfort to me!

When an infant messes his diapers, most parents quickly change the britches — for the good of the child and those around him. Otherwise his little bottom will eventually become irritated and raw, and pretty soon the aroma filtering throughout the room will be so offensive it will drive everyone out. We all realize an infant isn't capable of cleaning his own soiled diapers, but that doesn't make the odor any more pleasant to be around. It is still offensive! And when the diaper is finally changed it must be disposed of correctly or its odor will still permeate the room.

It is the same way when we sin. Sometimes, as babes in Christ, we need another's help in cleaning up, because if we continue to sit in that sin, that area of our lives becomes sore, irritated, and the adverse effects of sin encompass others around us. Soon, the whole place smells of the stench of sin. It must not only be cleaned up, but disposed of correctly.

Once we are born again, sin no longer has dominion over us. As we mature in the things of God, we should stop sinning. When we do sin, our heavenly Father never turns against us. Like my natural Dad, our heavenly Father takes full responsibility for us, but not our sin! We are still His sons, messy britches and all! And He is the best at cleaning up messes!

The Way Out Of Sin

Thank God for 1 John 1:9: **If we confess our sins, he is faithful and just to forgive us our sins, and to cleanse us from all unrighteousness.** It would be better if we didn't have to confess so frequently, if we didn't rebel against His Word and get into messes in the first place. But the way out of sin is there when we need it.

Everyone of us carries attitudes and lifestyles from our past into our Christian walk. While your inner man became a new creature in Christ the moment you were born again, it takes a while for your old man to catch up. Being made in the image of God, you are a three- part creature — spirit, soul, and body. Your soul, which consists of your mind, your will, and your emotions, takes a while to get the message! And slowest of all to catch the drift is your body.

In my case, I was like the "rebel without a cause," although, of course, *I* felt my causes were justified. I was so rebellious in my teenage years, my dad didn't know how to deal with me, so all he knew to do was to deal severely with me.

Because of the severe way Dad corrected me, I lost all respect for him, and I no longer trusted him. One night I became so resentful, I swore some day I would kill him. My vengeful mind spent weeks devising a plan, and I was thoroughly convinced I could kill him and nobody would ever discover who had done it.

It was my grandfather who talked me out of it, and brought me to my senses. He kept me from really messing my britches!

The Holy Spirit does the same thing for us that my grandfather did for me He teaches us all things and guides us into all truth. His desire is to keep us from sin by directing us to the principles of God's Word.

Cleaning Up the Mess

I was full of resentment, bitterness and unforgiveness toward my father. And, because I had lost all respect for my dad, the authority figure in my life, I had also lost all respect for his words. The problem was I carried this over into the spiritual realm as well. When I read in the Word that I should honor my father, I rebelled. I couldn't see how I could possibly submit to that Word. Finally, when the Holy Spirit dealt with me one day, I told God there just wasn't anything good in my dad to honor.

Then God spoke to me. "You're trying to honor him for what he's done, rather than for who he is." When I began to do this, honor him for who he was, not what he had done, my spiritual eyes were opened. And suddenly, I began to see some of the good he had done!

He taught me how to enjoy work.

He taught me how my word was my bond, so to be slow to give my word.

He taught me how to make good deals.

He taught me how to be aware of my surroundings — like when driving a car, looking four cars ahead and two cars behind — like when I walk into a room, to notice where furniture, people and doorways are.

Before this happened our relationship could only be classified as pitiful. I couldn't stand to be around Dad! I judged him by the things he had done to me in the past, and as far as I was concerned, the less I saw of, or thought about, him the better off I would be.

The Bible clearly states we are to forgive others, regardless of the offense. "If you do not forgive, neither will your heavenly Father forgive you your sins" (Matt. 6:15, author's paraphrase). Well, just as I rebelled against Dad's authority, I also wanted to rebel against that verse. In my rebellion, there was no room for forgiveness. I just plain didn't want to! I resisted like a scared kitten clings to a tree when he is in danger. Even if someone attempts to retrieve him, he clings desperately. If he would simply let go of the tree limb, he would be safe in the arms of his deliverer. But he is too scared to recognize that!

Sometimes we are the same way as that scared cat — afraid to let go of what ails us, even when we are in trouble! Many times pride stands in the way!

James 4:6 states, **But He gives more grace. Therefore He says: 'God resists the proud, but gives grace to the**

humble.' Therefore submit to God. Resist the devil and he will flee from you (NKJV).

There is a progression in those verses. First, we must put aside or confess pride. **Pride goeth before destruction, and a haughty spirit before a fall,** according to Proverbs 16:18. When we judge others, we are actually operating in pride, setting ourselves up as God himself. James 4:12 says, **There is one lawgiver, who is able to save and to destroy: who art thou that judgest another?** Romans 14:12: **So then everyone of us shall give account of himself to God. Let us not therefore judge one another anymore....**

Judging is not an option for the believer. When we judge someone else we usually attempt to elevate ourselves above them, even if we aren't consciously aware of it. We become self-righteous in our thinking. Since the Bible warns us about pride, that it leads to destruction, it pays us to heed that warning.

Submit, Then Resist

Once we have admitted our pride and confessed it as sin, only then can we truly humble ourselves before God. We do this by agreeing with God's Word, His authority. He gives grace to the humble, His all-sufficient grace that enables us to deal with any situation. Do you realize we need grace to even submit ourselves entirely to God? And we need it to resist the devil! His Word here promises *more* grace to those who humble themselves!

Most of the time we are trying to resist the devil before we submit ourselves to God! So we go about the whole messy britches thing backwards! Did you ever try to change a messy diaper when the baby was lying on its stomach? No, that is upside down and backwards! It won't work!

Once I admitted pride in judging my dad, allowing God to be God in his life, then I could truly humble myself before Him, submit to the Word and see Dad for *who* he was, not for what he had done. Resisting the devil concerning my feelings towards Dad was no longer an issue. *"Flee"* means "to run away," "vanish," "escape."[1] We could say that *to flee* would mean to run away in absolute terror — and that is what the devil does when we honor the Word, submit to God, resist the devil, and walk in our authority!

Honoring Dad wasn't enough, however, because I still had to forgive him. But forgiveness came easily once I saw him for who he was. God does the same with us. He loves us, yet hates the sin. I hated what my dad had done to me when I was younger, but once I realized I could separate him from his actions, forgiveness was easy.

We forgive by faith choosing, as God does, not to remember the sin again. You may wonder why I have just recounted my dad's actions if I truly had forgotten them. Well, God *chooses* not to remember, he doesn't just *forget.* Yet, as examples to us, He has recorded many of our Bible heroes' sins, hasn't He? He is not mad at them, nor does He hold their sins against them anymore. He wants us to learn from them, to recognize that even the greatest of men have all sinned and come short of the glory of God.

When I think of what Dad did to me, how severely he punished me, I realize now that he didn't know what he was doing. If you had asked him years later, he couldn't have even recalled those times. There is no longer any hurt, bitterness or resentment on my part for his past actions. They are forgiven, just as God forgives us.

One thing that really helps us forgive is to realize that we do it by faith. Feelings may not be there at first. But feelings will always follow our actions. By faith, we apply the love of God shed abroad in our hearts by the Holy Spirit. This love isn't a feeling, but a decision on our part to believe and act! We must act on our faith or it will die. **Faith without works is dead** (James 2:17). When we take the appropriate or corresponding actions, by faith, death departs in that area, and life comes! Glory!

The Extra Mile

Blessing the person you have forgiven also helps the feelings. When God forgives he restores us to right standing — just as if it had never happened. No longer do we need to wallow in guilt, condemnation, inferiority or any sense of sin. If we forgive God's way, we will treat the person as if they had never sinned against us. Blessing them in some way brings this into reality in our hearts, as well as theirs.

In some cases, simply praying for the person who has offended you will restore them in your heart to right standing. Other times you may want to do something specific to show them your love, your forgiveness. They may never know the extent of your former feelings towards them, but it sure will help you to bless them. It seals the deal, so to speak, in your heart. It puts action to your faith! I challenge you to do this!

In 1993, my dad went on to be with the Lord. I am so glad God changed my heart long before then. My relationship with Dad was marvelous in his last years. He moved to Tulsa, where I live, a few years ago because of poor health. He could no longer work, and needed me to take care of him. One morning, as we sat in a Waffle House eating breakfast, he said, "After all these years that I've taken care of everyone, bailed them out on a continual basis, now I have to place myself in your hands for your care and keeping."

We sat there and just bawled like a couple of babies as we thought how events had changed between us. Dad had taken care of me, cleaned up my messy britches for so many years, and now it was my turn to take care of him. How dreadful it would have been if forgiveness hadn't already been established in my heart, and God's love restored between us.

When I was in town I visited Dad every day, or called him on the phone. And even though I took care of him financially, he was always giving to me. When I gave him my car he gave me his old truck. I loved it! I fixed it up and even today have great fun in it! But the fun that truck brings me cannot compare to the joy that is mine because I got free from all bitterness and unforgiveness towards Dad. It pays to obey God! Joy unspeakable, full of glory comes when we obey His Word.

Psalm 119:9: **How can a young man cleanse his way? By taking heed according to your word** (NKJV). When I finally took heed to His Word, paid attention to it, my old ways with Dad were cleansed. Just like taking a bath, the water was there all the time in the pipes, the soap in the soap dish, and the shower stall empty, bidding me to come on in! Once we have experienced a hot, steaming shower we feel so much better. In the spiritual realm, the water of the Word washes us clean; we emerge refreshed and restored, free from the sin and condemnation that accompanies it. And then we wonder why we waited so long!

Psalm 119:11: **Your word I have hidden in my heart, that I might not sin against You** (NKJV). Here is the important ingredient to eliminate sin in our lives — keeping His Word hidden in our hearts.

Verse 10 of Psalm 119 says, **With my whole heart have I sought You; oh, let me not wander from your commandments!** (NKJV). If we seek Him entirely, with all that is within us, with our whole heart, then we wouldn't need cleansing so often, would we? The reason I wandered from Dad's commands was I didn't seek loving him. I chose to withhold respect, because I considered my reasons justified. And yet, I know how Dad loved me all the time, he just didn't know how to deal with me effectively. And he didn't know how to show his love to me back then.

When you love someone wholly, you cherish every word they have ever spoken to you.

With my lips I have declared all the judgments of Your mouth. I have rejoiced in the way of Your testimonies as much as in all riches. I will meditate on Your precepts and contemplate Your ways. I will delight myself in Your statutes. I will not forget Your word.

Psalm 119:13-16 NKJV

That man is speaking of an all-out love affair between God and himself.

With Your Whole Heart

I am reminded of a man who is hopelessly in love with a woman. He pursues her with everything he has. He hangs on his sweetheart's every word, speaks of her all the time, loves her more than anyone or anything else in the world. He thinks about her constantly, his world is immersed in her, because he is totally dedicated to love her and her alone. Unfaithfulness is out of the question.

Now that is how God wants us to be with Him! I realize thinking about it in this natural vein can seem crude by comparison, but if you have ever felt that way about a woman, you get my point!

Any man who treats a woman that way is bound to succeed with her. And anyone who follows this psalm's instruction is sure to be successful in all his endeavors. Why? Because he makes the right choices, right responses along the way.

First, he cleanses his ways by paying quick attention to the Word, taking his shower when needed. *Second,* he seeks God wholly, with his heart, not his head. *Third,* he hides

God's Word in his heart, so he will remain faithful and stay out of trouble.

He is also teachable, desirous of really knowing godly principles. He speaks constantly of the goodness of God, and rejoices in His words. God is first in his life, more valuable than any riches. He thinks God's ways, delights himself in God's Word, and chooses never to forget it, no matter what the circumstances.

That kind of man is a joy to be around — he is clean, smells and looks good and influences others to stay that way! Mama was right, it *is* smart to take a bath! But it is wiser still to stay clean! It may not be possible with our natural bodies because they are bound to get dirty along the way, but in the Spirit realm, if we follow the Word, we will remain spotless by the Blood of the Lamb!

5
Help, My Emotions Are Showing!

Growing up in East Texas, certain images of manhood were imprinted on my mind which have been difficult to erase. John Wayne was the stereotype of a "real man" and "real men don't cry" was the phrase of the day.

Men back then were rough and ready, never tender and sensitive. In the West, where "men were men and wimmin' were wimmin'," the men brought home the bacon while the women stayed home and cooked it. Male bonding was unheard of and we certainly didn't go off in the woods with a bunch of guys to beat drums and howl!

Male and female roles were well defined, although not always in keeping with Biblical principles. As a result I carried certain ideas into my marriage that were wrong and my family suffered for it.

I tried to be the strong one, the tough guy with all the answers. The problem was I didn't even understand the questions!

The first few years of our marriage after our daughters were born were pure hell. I never showed them any real affection, even though I loved them dearly. I didn't realize they needed tenderness and attention from their father. Even if I had known it then, my own personal frustrations hindered me from really opening myself to them.

I considered housework and child care "woman's work" and wouldn't even consider changing the babies' diapers. I ordered my family around like a drill sergeant and expected them to jump whenever I barked out the orders. It is a wonder Pat remained married to me, but I thank God she did.

Now I realize how differently men and women function, particularly in the soulish realm. I could have saved my family a lot of grief had I known it back then.

I just thought Pat's sensitivity and tears on occasions when I was rough with her were her way of manipulating me. That is what I had been taught. I didn't realize women were so affected by what they heard. I didn't realize she needed love words from me. "Why can't she just be logical, like me?" I would ask myself when she got upset and cried. "Why does she have to resort to emotionalism just because I've yelled at her for the past two days?"

So many men consider women to be fluffballs because of their sensitivity and yet, God designed them to be sensitive and intuitive. Let's look at the two words used in Genesis for man's and woman's creation.

Genesis 2:7: **And the Lord God formed man of the dust of the ground, and breathed into his nostrils the breath of life; and man became a living soul.** That word *formed* means "squeezing into shape...to mould into a form; especially as a potter"[1] — formed as a potter would a piece of clay. I can see it now — God reached down to the earth, picked up some clay and formed or squeezed that clay into a man's form. When it says He **breathed...the breath of life** into Adam's nostrils, it literally states in the Hebrew, "breath of lives."[2] He actually breathed two lives into man — for woman was within him, soon to be created in a different manner.

Woman's creation was so different from man's in the beginning. Verse 22 of Genesis 2 states, **And the rib, which the Lord God had taken from man, made he a woman, and brought her unto the man.** Keeping in mind that man was *molded*, or squeezed into shape, in his formation, we now discover that woman was *made*. She wasn't squeezed into shape, but *made* — she was skillfully and carefully hand-crafted. Just as a skillful craftsman would create a delicate crystal vase, so God created woman, a totally unique being, yet completely complementary to man. She was refined to perfection for God's man on the earth, from man himself rather than directly from the dust of the earth.

We will discuss further in the section on husband/wife relationships the necessity for men to recognize fully what a precious gift God has given him in his wife, but right now let's simply consider the soulish differences, particularly in the emotions.

A Physical Basis

Scientists have discovered that the male brain is different from the female brain. During fetal development, around the sixteenth week in a mother's womb when the male organs are positioning, the chromosomes in his brain also change, affecting the communication links between the right and left hemispheres of his brain. Now he no longer has the same ability to communicate freely his feelings as females do, who have both sides of their brain easily accessible. Thus, the male becomes more logical in his approach to life. It is not that he doesn't have emotions, but because of the reduced chromosome link between the left and right hemisphere of his brain, he isn't as easily in touch with them, nor can he easily communicate his feelings.

This fact alone brings major problems in a marriage if not understood. It seems women can so easily explain how they feel, and they expect men to do likewise. They are usually more tender and sensitive, unless they have been abused in childhood. It is not typical for them to think logically first about everything. They tend to approach life with their emotions. Certainly, we can understand God's purposes in creation. If women and men thought alike, life would not only be dull, but why would man need woman? If they were both very logical, and unable to show emotions fully, wouldn't their children suffer from a real lack of affection and care?

It has been said that a woman's mind functions like a computer. Volumes of information are placed within and when the right buttons are pushed, out comes a certain response, although she doesn't always know just how she arrived at her conclusions. The world sometimes calls it woman's intuition. This is not merely a spiritual discernment, their intuition is usually right. For instance, have you ever noticed that upon making a new acquaintance, perhaps someone who has impressed you greatly, your wife will say something like this: "Honey, I just don't trust them!" When asked, she may or may not know why, but months later you find out she was right all along! It is downright frustrating how right they can be sometimes! Especially when it comes to judging an individual's character.

The male brain functions more like a manually operated adding machine. Information is fed into it, one item at a time as the handle is pulled down to register each amount. Slowly, as information accumulates, a receipt or ticket is printed, eventually adding everything up and producing a grand total. Unlike the computer, the conclusion can be easily read and understood. Everything is right there before you. You can see all the facts on paper. There is no question as to how the conclusions were calculated. Men function like that — they are a little slower at understanding their feelings regarding things, or their appraisal of others, but when they do decide something, they usually have logical reasons for their conclusions.[3]

So we are both fearfully and wonderfully made, with different functions for different purposes. But in order to relate to others, we men must learn to communicate feelings, not just facts. We must display emotions, and not just when we are angry. Our wives and children need affection, not logic, when they are hurting. They need understanding when they are discouraged, not facts. They need to feel loved when they have been misunderstood by others, not criticism. Sometimes they just need to be held, not ignored when they feel insecure. And we need to talk to them so they can minister to our needs appropriately.

Jesus, Our Example

If you study the ministry of Jesus, you will see He was a man of emotions, and He was not afraid to show them. Jesus cried with remorse when His friend, Lazarus, died. He displayed infinite tenderness towards the woman taken in adultery. He was moved with compassion for hungry multitudes who followed Him, ministering to their needs, physically and spiritually. He took children gently into His arms and loved them. On the cross, in the midst of His agony, He showed His utmost love for His mother as He instructed John to care for her.

Other emotions were also evident in Jesus' life. He displayed intense anger when the money changers cheated the temple worshippers. His frustration showed when His own disciples were doubtful and unbelieving. His revulsion for hypocritical actions of religious leaders was evident on several occasions. And in the garden of Gethsemane the emotional torture He experienced was so great, He sweat great drops of blood. Now that is anguish of the soul!

Isaiah describes Jesus as **a man of sorrows** (Isa. 53:3). When He travailed in the garden, His agony came from yielding His will to the Father's will. Perhaps He realized His separation from the Father, as He took on the sins of the world, would be almost unbearable. The stress was so great, the mental anguish so intense, that He bled. The fact that blood was shed during emotional agony should bring us great comfort in our own times of stress, whatever the cause.

He was a man of sorrows who understands what we go through. He shed His cleansing and healing blood for us that night even before going to the cross. His was not natural blood, but supernatural, coming directly from His heavenly Father. Our bloodline is established from our earthly father. His was precious, redeeming blood, sacrificed, shed for our mental health and well-being.

We need to be honest as men and recognize we have feelings too. Just because access to those feelings is different, sometimes difficult, for us, doesn't excuse our tendency to ignore them. Ignoring them simply shows our ignorance! The apostle Paul didn't ignore his feelings in times of distress. He wrote of the hardships he endured, and of God's delivering grace in those hard times. His intense zeal for God was often misunderstood and disliked. His preaching was rejected by many of his Jewish brethren, and they retaliated severely.

But, rather than hide his feelings, Paul revealed them, because he understood the comfort of God, and realized his words would comfort others for ages to come. **Blessed be God...the God of all comfort**, he wrote in 2 Corinthians 1:3. *The Amplified Bible* words this verse: **...the God [Who is the Source] of every comfort (consolation and encouragement).** Another translation says that He is the God of unlimited encouragement! I like that!

Further in that same chapter, Paul described times when he needed this comfort.

> **For we would not, brethren, have you ignorant of our trouble which came to us in Asia...insomuch that we despaired even of life: But we had the sentence of death in ourselves, that we should not trust in ourselves, but in God which raiseth the dead; Who**

delivered us from so great a death, and doth deliver, in whom we trust that he will yet deliver us....
2 Corinthians 1:8-10

One paraphrased version of verse 8 reads, **Our stress was so great we could snap at any time.** I can identify with that kind of stress — I have been there before! Like Paul, I have recognized trusting in myself is useless. Only God can deliver us in time of distress. Notice the tenses used in verse 10 — delivered, doth deliver, and will deliver — past, present and future. Jesus is the same yesterday, today and forever. God is my Source of unlimited encouragement. His delivering power is available at all times — whether I need it spiritually, emotionally or physically. He has delivered me in the past, He is doing it now, and He will continue to do so in the future!

David understood God's delivering power, having experienced it several times in his life. He knew God intimately and in his times of trouble we read how he poured his heart out to Him. David was called a man after God's own heart, meaning his heart was always seeking God's. He hungered after the things of God continually.

David also was in touch with his emotional needs. In fact, he didn't mind expressing them to God openly. Whether he was fearful or doubting, lonely, discouraged or troubled, he freely wrote his feelings in his psalms. But he always ended them in praise and adoration to God, acknowledging His strength and the fact that his deliverance came from Him.

David was honest with God. I believe because he could openly express his feelings to his Lord, he could readily receive help in his time of need. In times past we have preached faith to such an extent that people thought we should be completely exempt from feelings. Oh, it is true we can't depend on them, or be led by them, but we do need to identify them so we can properly deal with them.

And there is no point trying to con God — He knows how we feel anyway!

Men sometimes operate on the basis that only what others see or know about is known to God. On the surface it is easy to see through that bad logic. But, in reality, they are deceiving themselves into believing reality is only what others perceive to be true about them. They are hiding from themselves. Women, on the other hand often know us better than we do ourselves. That is why they are so good at giving us a reality check when we need it.

Did you ever realize that when Jesus told that rich young man to **love the Lord with all thy heart, and with all thy soul, and with all thy mind...** (Matt. 22:37), that He was including emotional love. It was not simply a spiritual thing. Our emotions are important — they are part of our souls, and they influence our minds. God wants us to love Him totally, with all of our being! But if we are full of anxieties and frustrations, if we are discontent or discouraged, we need to get those feelings out in the open before God, to cast our cares upon Him. Once we have done that, it is easier to obey Paul's exhortation in Philippians 4:4, **Rejoice in the Lord always!**

Victory Over Depression

Sometimes I have felt so low I simply couldn't rejoice, or at least, didn't want to. You have heard of someone being down to the bottom of the barrel. Well, I felt like I was under the barrel, with its bottom on top of me. At times like that I wanted to fall into self-pity, but feeling sorry for myself wouldn't help one bit. I know rejoicing will, but how do I get there?

Well, let's go back to the time when David was at Ziklag, as told in 1 Samuel 30. The Amalakites invaded David's camp, where he lived with 600 men, plus their wives and children. When David and his men returned from dealing with the Philistines, they found their camp burned down, their wives and children taken hostage by the Amalakites. They **lifted up their voice and wept, until they had no more power to weep** (30:4). Now notice what happens next. In their deep grief, David's men turned on him, blamed him for the whole mess and threatened to stone him to death. Do you know why? Because while they had wept before God, they didn't go the next step: they didn't seek God's deliverance or praise Him in the midst of their trouble. It is not enough just to vent our emotions, men, we must then do what the Word instructs. The only one in the group at Ziklag who did this was David!

Now put yourself in David's position. His home is destroyed by the enemy, his wives and children are missing, and now his own men turn on him, even talk of killing him. He was in trouble and hurting immeasurably. What would you do in his circumstance? Verse 6 tells us what David did. Even though he was greatly distressed, **...David encouraged himself in the Lord** (30:6). In other words, he put courage back into himself!

Can't you imagine how fear tried to jump on him, how discouraged he could have allowed himself to become? If ever a man could have gotten into a pity party (the kind of party no one else wants to attend!), it was David. But instead, he encouraged himself in the Lord. How did he do that? Well, we can see a pattern in David's life. Whenever he was in trouble, he cried out to God in psalms, then he began to praise God for his goodness and rejoice in his victory. He must have done that this day at Ziklag, after he had poured out his heart and wept until tears would come no more.

Then we are told he enquired of the Lord and found out how to pursue his enemy. Verse 19 says David recovered *all* that was stolen, **And there was nothing lacking to them, neither small nor great....**

I wonder if this chapter would have ended the same way had David simply wept and not encouraged himself, and not worshipped the Lord. I doubt it! In my own life, I have often identified with David. I have found myself on many occasions, literally singing my way back to emotional health and strength just as David did, just as Paul and Silas did in prison. When we rejoice and praise God the enemy flees and victory is ours!

When Paul told the Philippians to rejoice he knew how important it was to rejoice in all situations. His own circumstances were miserable! He had been arrested for preaching the Gospel and treated like a criminal!

Think about it, the word *re-joice*. When you are all out of joy, refuel on joy through rejoicing! The word *rejoice* has triple definitions. First, it means to grin really wide (which you do when you are filled with joy)! Then it means to jump up and down.[4] Thirdly, it means twirl around![5] Get the picture? Notice Paul doesn't say to rejoice when you feel good, or when things are going great. He says to rejoice *always!*

If you will do a study of other heroes in the Bible you will notice they all had "like passions," as any man. There is no need for us to live with the John Wayne mentality and never show our feelings. We can't honestly relate with God or others if we aren't open before them. In addition, we are likely to explode in anger, develop ulcers, or retreat into depression if we keep it all inside. God showed us the way to deal with them in His Word — we are to cast all our cares on Him and rejoice our way through it all. Now it is up to us to obey it, to be doers of the Word and not hearers only!

6
Living Sacrifice Or Dead Weight?

Have you ever had trouble keeping your body under control in some specific area? Have you given much thought to why that particular area is so tempting? There have been times when I thought things would be so much easier if I just didn't have to contend with my body and its fleshly desires. Now don't get too spiritual on me — everybody has to deal with some weaknesses in the flesh if you are alive and kicking.

What happens to you when you see a scantily clad woman flashed across your TV screen? Do you quickly turn it off, or watch for just a few seconds more, especially if there is no one else around. And what about a scrumptious hot fudge sundae that is suddenly set before you? Would it make any difference if you had a full meal two hours ago? If scantily clad women or hot fudge sundaes don't whet your appetite, something certainly does. Maybe it is the latest and hottest piece of new software or computer gadgetry, or how about a new car with leather seats? Understand, as long as the devil is on this earth, you are bound to be tempted in some area of your life. And if you yield to the temptation, by dwelling on it long enough, your actions will follow suit and your body will give in to the temptation, because your mind already has.

Remember, it is your mind that leads your body around, and not the reverse. Sometimes I felt like a big bull with a ring in its nose called "Temptation." All the Devil had to do was send one of his little imps along to give it a twist, and I would just follow along, knees buckled and eyes watering, right into the very temptation I so desperately wanted to avoid. It was maddening! But it wasn't my body that the devil would tweak, it was my mind. Like many of you, I was desperate to discover a way to successfully resist these attacks. I knew if I could resist the Devil he would flee from me, but I hadn't as yet found any effective method for resisting him.

I tried summoning all my will power and just gutting it out. It didn't work. I tried quoting Scripture at him; after all, that's what Jesus did. It also didn't work. I had folks I knew who had a closer walk with the Lord than I did pray for me, and even lay hands on me. That didn't help. I spent more time in the Word. I felt better, but still had no victory. In short, I had done everything I knew how to do to resist the Devil and still couldn't get that ring out of my nose. I was doing what I thought I saw Jesus do in Scripture, but it wouldn't work for me. What was I missing?

Then, I came across the key, and I would like to pass it on to you. It was there in Scripture all along, but I hadn't seen it. What I was missing was what Jesus did *before* he resisted the Devil.

Jesus made a complete surrender of Himself, spirit, soul and body, to the will of His heavenly Father — a *living sacrifice*. This positioned Jesus in His battle against the Devil, so that He could successfully resist.

The apostle Paul said the same thing to us in Romans 12:1: **I beseech you therefore, brethren, by the mercies of God, that ye present your bodies a living sacrifice, holy, acceptable unto God, which is your reasonable service.**

Living sacrifice — our bodies are to be living sacrifices, not dead weight! Oh, I have presented my body as a living sacrifice unto God so many times, but all too soon I found myself crawling off that altar when temptation struts itself in front of me.

But the next verse tells us how to keep that from happening. **And be not conformed to this world: but be ye transformed by the renewing of your mind, that ye may prove what is that good, and acceptable, and perfect, will of God** (12:2).

In reality, it is not our bodies that give us the problem, it is our carnal minds. Our body can't do anything on its own — our mind controls it — and thoughts control our minds. Therefore, if we change the way our minds operate we can overcome the attack of the enemy. But far too often, the enemy has been able to establish strongholds in our past, and these are the real culprits. Until our minds are renewed to the Word of God and those strongholds pulled down, our actions will fall into line with our wrong thinking instead of with God's Word.

The Game Plan

For though we walk in the flesh, we do not war after the flesh: (For the weapons of our warfare are not carnal, but mighty through God to the pulling down of strong holds;) casting down imaginations, and every high thing that exalteth itself against the knowledge of God, and bringing into captivity every thought to the obedience of Christ...

2 Corinthians 10:3-5

In the Greek, *stronghold* means "fortress."[1] A fortress is "a fortified place."[2] Like a fortress, strongholds keep us captive, as prisoners, until we pull them down, free ourselves from them. Our imagination is a powerful tool. It can be used by the Devil for evil, or we can use it for our good. I am reminded of an illustration in my own life which has spiritual principles involved, even though it is a natural illustration.

When I played football in high school my playing weight was only 154 pounds. I played guard against some big dudes, but this one time I had to play against this ol' boy who weighed 295 pounds. That is bigger than most college players. The coaches knew good and well that if I ever saw this guy I would have problems with my mind. They were absolutely right! So they began to program my mind with the right thoughts, so I would be victorious in this situation.

They told me, "Harrison, you'll come up against this big ol' boy, but you can take him! For one thing, you're quicker than he is." Well, I didn't have near as much to move! Then they said, "Not only that, but you can hit him real hard!" Well, I knew I was a hard hitter! Then they said, "When you come up and stand across from him in the line, don't look up. Look down at his hand, because you'll be right next to the center, where you can see the ball. That's the key, watching his hand and the ball." I knew what the count was, being on the offense, so when the ball was snapped I had to be ready, because his hand would go after the ball. Watching both, I could get that jump on him, and hit him before anything else could take place.

The only way they could sell me on my chances of beating this guy was to tell me the truth. If they had lied to me, I would have known better. They couldn't say, "You're bigger than him." That was a lie! There was no way they were going to get me to believe that. So if they were going to reprogram me, they had to do it with truth. The truth was I *was* quicker; the truth was I *could* hit harder. They told me the truth, and I could believe and accept it because it had already been proven.

OK, I was quick, and I hit hard, but he was still bigger. So they began to tell me he was slow. In fact, they said he was a pitiful player who just more or less occupied space. And we needed that space to run the ball!

So they got my mind ready. The game started with the kickoff, but I didn't see him running that time, which was just as well. But then, during that first play, I made a mistake — I looked up. Now they had told me don't look up at him because they knew what my mind would do. Right at that moment, my mind began to say, "No way, Jose!" In fact, I began to think, "If this fella wants this space, I will just give it to him!"

This was not the time to think defeat. I immediately looked down, and began to go through the thought patterns I had been taught. They said to look at his hand and watch the ball. They said the minute I heard the signal, go!

This is where a lot of Christians mess up. They don't listen to instructions and don't wait for the signals! Whether you know it or not, God calls some good signals. If you get in the rhythm of the count, and know the signal, you will win.

I was looking at that ball and watching his hand, listening for the signal. I had made up my mind that if I could, I was going to take his head off! That was the smallest part of him, so it seemed reasonable at the time! As big as he was, I had decided to take the smallest portion and go with it! I saw that ball move and I knew his hand was still on the ground. I fired with everything that was in me, I lunged at him, using my elbow and everything else I could find at that moment. I had made up my mind that I was going to get him. I popped him good, knocked his head back, and then his whole body went back. He ended up laying there on his back! Just as I thought: *The bigger they are, the harder they fall!* It sure felt good!

Now how did I ever handle such a big dude? His size could have become a stronghold but, instead, I had formed an image. I had seen myself whipping him, taking him, with thoughts, imaginations, which had been programmed in my mind from truth — I could hit harder; I was quicker! Jesus said, **Ye shall know the truth, and the truth shall make you free** (John 8:32). When you begin to think truth thoughts — truth that says, **Greater is he that is in you**

[me], **than he that is in the world** (1 John 4:4) — truth that says, **I can do all things through Christ which strengtheneth me** (Phil. 4:13), certain images become good strongholds within you. Those strongholds, or fortified places, help you keep your body from sin and sustain you in times of temptations, tests and trials.

The truth is a weapon that is mighty. It will pull down those wrong imaginations and help you keep your actions in line. Then those negative thoughts become your captives, instead of you being their captives! You bring them into captivity, make them your prisoners, keep them chained and bound from influencing you.

When I was a young man in the world I was taught certain things about women that were true, but could be used in perverted ways in certain circumstances. Women love to hear, "I love you," for example. Well, I grabbed hold of those truths, and used them to my advantage while I was still living in sin. I proved these truths effectively in my life, by my actions, but soon they took me captive.

It took the name of Jesus to break those chains of bondage, but I still had to walk in the greater truth, the Word of God. Otherwise, the old strongholds, worldly truths, would begin to affect my thinking again. If I let them affect my thinking, soon my imaginations would go wild again. Then I would find myself slipping back into those old patterns that I had once perfected. It is an area I must always guard. I keep my mind alert to the truth, which not only sets me free, but keeps me free! I can't allow my body to slip off the sacrificial altar and become dead weight, holding me down again.

Dead Men Don't Sin

Another truth that helped me greatly in keeping my body and actions under control is found in Romans 6:3-14. Verse 3 states we were baptized into Christ's death with

Him, and verse 6 states we were crucified with Him, that our old man with its body is free from serving sin. Now think about that — a dead man is free from serving sin. And if we are dead, how can we sin at all? A dead man is free from all of that.

Romans 8:2 states, **For the law of the Spirit of life in Christ Jesus hath made me free from the law of sin and death.** We are alive unto God and dead to sin. Sin should not reign in our bodies. That old man died with Jesus on the cross, and we have been raised to newness of life in Christ.

Neither yield ye your members as instruments of unrighteousness unto sin: but yield yourselves unto God, as those that are alive from the dead, and your members as instruments of righteousness unto God. For sin shall not have dominion over you: for ye are not under the law, but under grace.

Romans 6:13-14

Therefore, if sin is reigning over us, it is ruling us illegally because we are called to serve righteousness. And we do this, not as a legal matter, but by grace. We need to inform our bodies of this fact, that they cannot rule over us, but our new man, risen with Christ, is to rule over them through grace.

This is why staying in the Word on a regular basis is so critically important to being victorious. It keeps us constantly aware of the grace of God and our dependency upon it.

Grace is a term often misused and misunderstood. Most people define grace as God's unmerited favor, and that is an accurate definition, yet it can seem vague and incomplete. It doesn't really describe the fullness of grace. According to Ephesians 2:5, we are saved by grace, through faith. But God's grace continually works on our behalf, whether we deserve it or not, throughout our Christian walk. In fact, I need it more now than I ever did back when I was first saved, especially when it comes to keeping my body under control.

Paul wrote concerning grace to Timothy, a young minister who was a spiritual son to him. In 2 Timothy 2:1 he said, **Thou therefore, my son, be strong in the grace that is in Christ Jesus.** Timothy was struggling in his ministry when Paul wrote this. Now if one can be strong in grace, isn't it possible to be weak in grace? Why else would Paul have urged him to be strong in grace? Notice he didn't say be strong in will power? No, grace was something supernatural at Timothy's disposal and he was to be strengthened in it.

Kenneth Wuest's *Expanded Translation of the New Testament* states this verse differently: **As for you, therefore, my child, be clothed with the inward strength by the grace which is in Christ Jesus.** When someone is clothed in a garment, they must put that article of clothing on or slip into it. If it just hangs in your closet, it won't do you any good. You must wear it to get full use from it.

Charles Capps' definition of grace helped me understand the depth of grace better. He defined grace as God's willingness to operate on our behalf using all His power and abilities, even when we don't deserve it. *Grace* or *charis* has various meanings. Basically, it is "that which bestows...pleasure, delight, or causes favorable regard."[3] It speaks of God's merciful bounty, His blessings, His pleasures and joys designed just for us.

Hebrews 4:16 states that we are to come boldly into the throne of grace to obtain grace and mercy to help in our time of need. Therefore, we don't need to beg. Just as we walk into our clothes closet and put on a garment, so are we to walk into the throne of grace to receive, or put on grace and mercy. You don't hesitate to get clothes out of your closet when you need them, do you? No, you walk in there boldly, because it is your closet, and those clothes belong to you. It is the same with God's grace closet! Walk in and put it on! Walk in and obtain all of his power and ability! It belongs to you as a believer.

This is why regular time with God in prayer is also critically important. Prayer is the entrance into God's grace closet.

Paul did this in his famous "thorn in the flesh" episode.

> And lest I should be exalted above measure through the abundance of the revelations, there was given to me a thorn in the flesh, the messenger of Satan to buffet me, lest I should be exalted above measure. For this thing I besought the Lord thrice, that it might depart from me. And he said unto me, 'My grace is sufficient for thee: for my strength is made perfect in weakness.'
>
> Most gladly therefore will I rather glory in my infirmities,...in reproaches, in necessities, in persecutions, in distress for Christ's sake: for when I am weak, then am I strong.
>
> 2 Corinthians 12:7-10

Several things are evident here. First, the thorn was not a sickness but a satanic attack, a messenger of Satan sent to buffet him. To *buffet* means "to hit over and over again".[4] Paul was increasing in revelation, and when that happens, people do exalt you — even God exalts you! Satan was upset and attempting to squelch the revelations and the exaltations! If anyone gets praise and recognition he wants to be the one!

God never told Paul he wouldn't deliver him. In fact, later Paul said the Lord delivered him out of all his afflictions. What he did want Paul to realize was that in his own strength, he couldn't do it. And when he seemed at his weakest was when God's power, or *strength* as it says in the Greek, would take over. God was saying, "Paul, it's all at your disposal — my power is perfected in your weaknesses!"

When he said, "My grace is sufficient for any situation!" (v. 9, author's paraphrase), he meant sufficiency lacks for nothing — it fulfills the requirement, satisfies the present need, is adequate. God was saying "Hey, Paul, just lean on My grace. I know you're weak but that's OK, because My strength is perfected in your weakness. My grace will put you over, Paul; it will see you through!"

It is no wonder Paul could then "glory" in his troubles. All he had to do was recognize his own weakness and walk into his grace closet and put on all of God's ability and power, adequate enough for every situation!

Several years ago one of my staff was involved in an incredibly frustrating law suit. Legal papers had been filed to prevent him from exercising a good, moral and legal right of his. Not only did the papers contain out and out lies, twisted facts and unwarranted conclusions, but the opposing attorney got five continuances simply to get the case heard before a certain judge who was openly sympathetic with their point of view. In the natural there were only two chances of this staffer being victorious — slim and none.

This man and his wife went to prayer and called on the grace of God for their situation. Then they rehearsed the promises of God in the face of their adversity for more than six months. What was the result? In spite of the case being heard by that particular judge, the ruling went in favor of the staff member to such an extent that the judge went against his own history in such cases and awarded complete and total victory to the staffer.

God didn't leave Paul hanging on by his own strength, and He doesn't expect you to function that way either. In times of troubles, testings, temptations and trials, there is always God's sufficient grace to put you over, to give you victory. Your inabilities, your inadequacies, your weaknesses only make God's power more effective!

So when it looks like your body, with its ungodly desires that don't want to die, is going to take control — when those unwholesome thoughts try to bombard you day and night, when strongholds and imaginations rear their ugly heads, remember who you are and Who God is. Remember what His Word says about you, and replace those negative imaginations with the truth. Call upon God and put on God's grace, recognizing that each time you walk in that grace, you are becoming stronger in it! No, you may not be sufficient for the test, but God's grace will pass with ease every time it is put to test! It *is* sufficient!

* * *

In this first section we have explored some of the major themes of conflict challenging men today. But before we move on to the next section, dealing with being a husband, I want to make one final point. All we have discussed here is foundational to what comes in the next two sections. In other words, the biggest part of being a godly husband is being a godly man, and the biggest parts of being a godly father are being both a godly man and a godly husband.

When God builds a man, He does it the same way He does His church — line upon line, precept upon precept. (Isa. 28:10.) What is our job? To pay the price, make the effort, do the job, read the Word, make it work, be alert, not quit, not hide, not snivel, and most of all — never, never, never stop praying!

7
Husband Or Has Been?

Actually, I feel Pat has been a far better wife than I have been a husband. As a godly woman, she learned most of her truths from the Word. Being raised in a good, loving home, she was encouraged to be a doer of the Word. Most of what I have learned was through mistakes I made, so I am encouraging you not to make the same mistakes. Don't fall into the same pits I did.

I can't tell you I have all the answers or know everything. But when you have lived some years in this life, there are things you just stumble upon. I have discovered a few things I want to point out.

Through the years I have seen that God's Word is full of tremendous truths to aid me in ministering to my wife's needs. Did you notice that I referred to meeting my wife's needs as a ministry? The first thing you must see is that you have ministry at home. We have all been told we have a ministry of reconciliation to the world, but first comes your ministry at home. You need to see it as such, so you can fulfill it.

Not only are you to meet your wife's needs but this should be your first priority. So often we give so much attention to raising our children, but after that is completed, it is still going to be just you and Mama! You start with her, and you are going to finish with her, so no matter what happens during the time when the children are there, or anything else that is going on in your life, your ministry to her is still number one.

Understand I am speaking of things in the natural when I say your wife is your number one ministry. Spiritually speaking, your first ministry is to the Lord, but in the home, your wife is first.

Many ministers place their wives and children way down on their list of "real ministry." They ignore their own family's needs, but seek to save the entire world. If they are not careful, they lose their families in the process! Some people can be really bold witnesses at work, but I have news for you. Your first bold witness should be at home to your wife and children — they see you as you really are!

Getting A Good Start

Most newly married men start out sincerely wanting to be good husbands. In many cases, they accomplish that by trial and error. Entering marriage unprepared, they usually know little about women and far less about what God's Word says about marriage. Nine times out of ten, we have looked to our fathers as role models, and many of them weren't too swift! Then we end up with a poor image of what a husband is supposed to be and frustration sets in. Once that frustration sets in, we wind up being more of a "has been" than a husband!

Oh, you may still be married to the same woman, but after the first year or two of trying, you probably gave up on "giving it your all." You may be living in the same house, going by the same name, but emotionally you are apart. There is no longer any joy in the relationship, and you are simply going through the motions. You may be still married, but emotionally you are divorced.

Maybe you are at a place in your marriage where you want out, or possibly you are discouraged trying to understand your wife. Maybe you are a wounded husband, with scars to prove it, and your only reason for staying in the marriage is your children's welfare, or because you know God hates divorce. Those are no reasons to stay together. We need to be staying together because it is the right thing to do, according to the Word!

I think all newlyweds start out with stars in their eyes — with the idea that everything is going to be grand and glorious and wonderful, and they are going to have nothing but wonderful times. Then the first few things go wrong, things they don't like, and they begin to falter because their hearts haven't been illuminated by God's Word.

Some newly married folks figure once they marry the one they wanted with all their heart, they will also *automatically* get everything else they ever wanted out of a marriage relationship. Nothing could be further from the truth. A good marriage is a work of artistry. Emphasis on work!

Maybe you are a newlywed with stars in your eyes and wonder on your face. Maybe your marriage is good, but you want it to be better. Whatever your circumstances, I believe God's Word will illuminate your heart and bring you better understanding and strength to become the husband He intends you to be.

To understand God's purpose for marriage we need to go back to the beginning. In Genesis 2:18 God said, **It is not good that the man should be alone....** Notice He didn't say anything about women being alone, but most women will tell you it is equally important for them not to be alone. Actually, I think women in general are smart enough to know they don't want to be alone. Sometimes it takes us men a little while to catch up in our understanding of how important it is to have that one true helpmeet.

Even though God came into the garden and fellowshipped with Adam, walked and talked with him, Adam still needed more than God for it to be "good." God considered Adam to be alone on this earth without another human being to enjoy, to love. Animals failed to meet the requirements! Man had needs that only another human being could meet, so God said He would make him a helpmeet.

A Helpmeet

Basically, the word *helpmeet* means one who aids or surrounds with aid and assistance.[1] God had given Adam a job in the garden. He was to **dress it and to keep it** (Gen. 2:15). He was to take charge, use his God-given dominion, guard it, protect it and tend the natural elements within it. But God didn't want Adam to do it alone — so He sent Adam the world's first ministry of helps department, wrapped up in a beautiful package, and suitable to aid and assist him in the garden. God had given Adam a ministry here on earth, but didn't want him to be alone in that ministry.

If you don't understand God's intentions, you will say, "Yeah, I knew my wife was here to help me." But ask yourself, why did Adam need help, and just what did he need aid and assistance in?

I have never read anywhere that Eve shoveled up hippopotamus manure while Adam sat on a bale of hay, sipping lemonade. No, it wasn't just the domestic labor or physical assistance that woman was to bring to man!

In our macho society, with our warped mentality, we sometimes react out of past patterns handed down to us. In some countries men are extremely dominant, and yet other countries or cultures develop a matriarchal society where women dominate. Sometimes the pendulum can swing from one extreme to the other. But it was never intended that either man or woman should be the head honcho!

The man has the responsibility for being the head (we will get into that in a later chapter), because he was created first. However, it was meant for both of them to be involved, to come to a place of unity where they could assist and balance one another and function as one flesh. We need to have men who will be men, who will let their women be women, and both work together as a team!

Let's look at another definition for helpmeet. It means "one who stands in the front of and looks into the eyes of."[2] The expression "eye to eye" originated here. Adam and Eve only had eyes for one another; there was agreement, oneness. They were one flesh, a perfect union. When you look into someone's eyes you can see a reflection of yourself. Wouldn't that be oneness; wouldn't that be unity? What happens when you look into your wife's eyes? You should see yourself, because you are one.

Adam didn't need Eve's assistance so much to help him do what he was charged to do, but rather, to discover, become and fulfill who he was designed to be.

Not only were they to be eye to eye, but the word *helpmeet* also means "alter-ego."[3] A man has to have an ego, a center inside himself that feels strong and self-confident. If he doesn't, he is never going to accomplish anything; he will never have any drive, always being a back-seat person. Without a healthy ego he is going to be run over by circumstances, and possibly his wife. One of the things a wife provides in surrounding and assisting him is a nurturing environment for his ego in a positive way.

My wife feeds my ego, and I thank God for her! Let's face one thing, men. Whether we are talking about just doing things around the home, or we are in bed, or in our business, we want our wives to look at us and say, "You're terrific!" or "Honey, you're a stud!" or "You're the best!" We may all use different terminology, but in essence, that is what we want to hear.

Is there anything wrong with that? No, godly husbands are supposed to be taking the lead, and when your wife feeds your ego, as your alter-ego, she is lending support at a very fundamental level. When she does, we feel like we can do anything. When she doesn't, we drop below the level where you are most effective. We don't reach for that accomplishment. This is an area I need Pat's help in just like you do from your wife. I need my wife telling me, "You're a dude, you're something else — if anybody can do it, you can!"

It may puff me up like a toad but, bless God, it can also get me to reach down inside myself and pull out that full effort to get it done! It is not a lot different than you complimenting your wife on how she looks to you, to keep her self-confidence level flying high. It makes her better able to relate to you and her world as well.

Why It Is The Way It Is

On any given day most any team can beat most any other team in their league. But, more often than not, the victory goes to whichever team is more psyched up and ready that day — the team, or individual, who has the self-confidence and ego strength to get the job done. The same thing holds true when it comes to being what we ought to be as men in the earth. Until we get psyched up to do it, we don't have the ego to pull it off. We will sit back and watch somebody else do it. For us to be men and husbands like we need to be, we have to have a wife who surrounds us with aid and assistance in the context of that reflection relationship — that eye to eye relationship where your ego is built up.

Something I do that helps my ego, and my wife's as well, is to dress my wife as best I can. When I see her all dressed up, I think, *Ain't she something to look at!* That pumps me up. It irks me to see preachers who look like they have stepped out of the band box, while their wives look like they have been to the Goodwill store. That tears me up, and it would destroy my ego. I want to fix her up. I would have rings hanging off every finger of hers. She enjoys it so much I got concerned one time that she was going to grow more fingers!

In Genesis 2:23 Adam said, **This is now bone of my bones, and flesh of my flesh: she shall be called Woman because she was taken out of Man.** Even though Adam slept while God created woman, he instinctively knew she was part of him; she was his other half. Here was someone made expressly for him, yet so uniquely different.

The word *ribs* here is translated "beams" in other parts of the Bible.[4] It denotes strength. Beams hold up buildings, aid and assist in the strength of a building whether they are seen or not. Whether you know it or not, your wife aids and assists you in strength. You must see that as her place, to strengthen you, because you need that. Others might not see it, but it is important for you to recognize and utilize her assistance and strengths.

I can be questioning myself in my mind, my attitudes, my motives and everything else. Then I will lie in bed at night with my wife and we will start talking. She will begin to share with me, and by the next day I am ready. I am strong enough to make a decision. You may say, "Brother you must be weak." Well, yes, I am bound to be, otherwise why would I need strength?

Why is it, as macho men, we can't ever admit weakness. What does the Bible say? **Let the weak say I am strong** (Joel 3:10). What we were doing is calling those things that be not as though they were. So we are weak, and don't sit there and think you never have those weak moments. You are lying to yourself if you do that. You need the strength she brings you. She is part of building your home and your family. That is why I want to hear what Pat has to say. She brings me strength and aids and assists me in becoming all God wants me to be.

The word *ribs* also means "chamber."[5] In Genesis 1:27 when God created man in his image, He created him **male and female created he them**. I believe the rib was, in actuality, a chamber containing woman's female parts or characteristics because, according to one source, the word *woman* used in Genesis 2:23 means "out of the womb of man." Men don't normally have wombs! So God put Adam to sleep, removed the inner chamber of him, skillfully creating this lovely hand-crafted female. A piece of art, a beautiful piece of art. How many of you know beauty is in the eye of the beholder? But beauty is not just the physical, it is the whole being, spirit, soul and body. If you always look at beauty being just physical, you will end up being frustrated in life.

Beauty doesn't start with the physical — it ends with the physical. It starts with the spirit. When a woman is born again, filled with the Holy Ghost, alive unto God, she is beautiful, no matter what that house, her body, looks like. And when her soul (her mind, her will and emotions) are affected by the Word of God, her beauty radiates even more. Beauty within will radiate without, and whether it measures up to what the world considers a "10" or not, the beauty is still obvious to you.

We have got to put first things first: spirit, then soul, then body. To those of us who grew up in a carnal world as I did, my idea of beauty was strictly physical. However, I soon found that my wife was far more beautiful inwardly than she was outwardly.

Adam found completion in Eve as his helpmeet. She was all that he was not — the soft, feminine side of mankind. She was also the more emotional side, the one to encourage him to fulfill God's plan for his life. She was to be his best friend, his companion, his assistant, his completer.

Helpmeet in Business

Harrison House would not be complete today if Pat had not been my completer. She was my friend who told me the

78

truth, who kept me going when I wanted to quit, when I doubted myself. I remember one time when Harrison House was really young, we had been embezzled of $20,000. We were at crossroads. The company was only about two years old and, in those days, we lived from book to book regarding publishing and distribution. I got so frustrated in the process that I questioned whether God had even told me to start the company or not. I was facing a great dilemma.

I had called the company Harrison House because God had said, "I've given you a good name, and I want to use it." Now when this challenge came, I got confused. Was this just something I had done on my own? Was this just a big ego trip I was on? Have you ever become confused and just lost your confidence in everything you were doing? I was in a tailspin and couldn't think straight, so I decided, bless God, I am going to talk to Brother Hagin. He is a prophet of God, and I am going to get the Word of the Lord from him. I believe what the Bible says, **Believe ye God's prophets, so shall ye prosper** (2 Chron. 20:20). I wanted to prosper, so I set my will to believe what he would tell me.

I went to him and explained the situation. Then I said, "I need to hear from you right now, as the man of God. When I started Harrison House, was that ego — was I out there on my own — was that my flesh? Because if so, I need to kill this thing right now. I need to let it die, bury it, forget about it and go do something else. If it was God, I need to stand and fight for it." "Brother Hagin," I continued, "I don't need you to take three weeks to pray about this. I've got to know something right now."

He didn't hesitate. Immediately he looked at me and boldly said, "I don't know. You'll have to decide that." I thought, *Here I am willing to believe the prophet and he tells me I will have to decide.* I felt even worse.

I went back and told Pat what he had said. "Honey," she replied, "I can remember when God spoke to you about it. I remember what He said." She started recounting one fact after another. I couldn't remember any of it at that moment because I couldn't think straight, but I said, "OK, I know you wouldn't lie to me, so I am going to act on it even though I don't feel like it." Harrison House still exists today because I had a wife who surrounded me with aid and assistance and was that supporting beam of strength to me. She got eye to eye with me and told me truth.

God wants to have a face-to-face relationship with man, and He wants us to have a face-to-face relationship with our wives. I am not too proud to recognize my need for Pat, especially in the area of telling me the truth — the truth sets you free. (John 8:32.) I was free to go on until today, years later, because she got eye to eye with me and told me the truth. I am still benefiting from it. I owe her a lot. She deserves every dress I can give her, every piece of jewelry I can put on her. She has done so much for me — we are one flesh.

Husbanding 101

Now that we have established the need for a wife, what is it we need to be as husbands? Ephesians 5:25 gives us a glorious description of Christ and the Church, instructing husbands and wives to be likewise. **Husbands, love your wives, even as Christ also loved the church and gave himself for it....**

He has given us a pattern here. Did you notice He said for husbands to give *themselves?* — not just money, not just time, not just things, but we must be willing to give ourselves? To give yourself there has to be an element of trust. *Why?* Because we become vulnerable when we give ourselves.

Many men are afraid they will be used, abused and taken advantage of. (No, this is not just something females have problems with.) That is why it is so important to build friendship within your marriage — because you can trust a true friend. And truth is at the basis of real friendship; it must prevail between you.

Sometimes I may not want to hear the truth from my wife, but I know she will tell me anyway. Always hearing the truth from her keeps our friendship at a level where I can feel safe. I know she will tell me the truth not only because I need it, but also because it is in my best interests, as her husband and her friend, for her to do so. Since we are one flesh it is also in her best interests too.

Consider the following job description out of Ephesians 5:26-30.

That he might sanctify and cleanse it with the washing of water by the word, that he might present it to himself a glorious church, not having spot, or wrinkle, or any such thing; but that it should be holy and without blemish.

So ought men to love their wives as their own bodies. He that loveth his wife loveth himself. For no man ever yet hated his own flesh; but nourisheth and cherisheth it, even as the Lord the church: For we are members of his body, of his flesh and of his bones.

What a privilege we have as husbands to be compared to Jesus, to have His pattern set before us. But what a challenge we have set before us: to relate to our wives as He related to the Church. The Word says, **As He is so are we, in this world** (1 John 4:17). However, we don't have to do it in our own strength and with only our wisdom. By example Jesus clearly shows us how to minister to our wife's needs, *and* we have supernatural abilities because we are more than mere men!

When we begin to see ourselves as how God has created us to be, it changes our whole view of our mates and our relationship to them.

The first ministry we have to our wives is that of prayer. Jesus' present-day ministry is praying for us, for **He ever liveth to make intercession for them** [the saints] (Heb. 7:25). Notice, men, I didn't say preach to them, or try to change them, but pray for them. When observing their weakness, their faults, you are to take those to the Father in prayer, not criticize them. Ephesians 5:26 shows us how Jesus does it — by washing of the Word. When you pray the Word of God over your wife daily, you are effectively washing her with the Word.

It occurs to me that many men will gladly give to their wives in many other ways than prayer. They will hand over the paycheck; they will help with the housework; they will take her shopping, even baby-sit the kids and give her a free Saturday now and then. But the question is: will they pray for her daily? All those other things are good, but if you don't pray for her daily, the other things aren't worth much! The pattern is there in the Word — He lives to make intercession for us — therefore, if we are going to be like Him, and He is praying continually for the Church, then we have to be praying regularly for our wives.

Also, when we pray for our wives, our motives must to be pure. In the past I have caught myself praying for Pat so she would be what I wanted her to be. Being raised in a gambler's home, I learned a lot of things sexually that the average wife isn't going to know or have any desire to participate in. So I had these old carnal desires that had been inbred in me (not that sexuality shouldn't be alive and exciting for Christians). There *should* be an ecstacy that goes beyond what the world has to offer, but my desires were selfish.

When I started praying for Pat, I would say, "God, she's your child, so you tell her she ought to do this for me...." It is just like my prayers bounced right back at me. I would be thinking, "God, you said, you would give me the desires of my heart. I've got these desires I want satisfied, and my saying things to her won't do any good. I am asking you, Lord, speak to her heart, change her." Great frustration set in because I didn't see any changes, and I found the longer I prayed that way, the more frustrated I got.

What God wanted was for me to change my attitude. I had to have a willingness to conform to his image, to change my old raunchy ideas. In praying for her, God wanted me to pray His will, not my will. If I pray His will, then His will gets done and we will both wind up being satisfied. Selfishness must go in order for God's will to be accomplished.

Marriage is a covenant agreement, and it means giving your all, one hundred percent, to the other. Whether you recognize it or not at the time, you died to independent living when you married your wife — or you should have! I don't know why it is that women love to shop. I am almost certain they invented the whole situation. And why they want their husbands, who would much rather stay home and watch Saturday afternoon football games, to accompany them on the shopping jaunts is beyond me.

If you accompany your wife on her shopping trips, that is sacrificial giving! But think of it this way: if she is shopping for her own clothes and you are helping her select what looks best on her, you are accomplishing Ephesians 5:27, "presenting her a glorious woman" (author's paraphrase), even as Christ presents a glorious Church. Sometimes we have to look at the practical side of the Scriptures. I understand that verse is referring to spiritual matters, but essentially, it says Christ wants His church to look great, to have all His abundant glory on display. So when you clothe your wife in nice things, you are doing likewise. That ought to make paying out the money a little easier on your mind.

Notice that this passage also mentions not having spot or wrinkle. Spots are sins which should be taken care of in prayer. The word *wrinkle* here means "dried up and burdened."[6] Even though **spot** and **wrinkle** in Ephesians 2:27 refers to the Church, we can draw an analogy to women, and women don't get this way overnight. Wrinkles come from worry, from fretting, anxieties, mistrust, from stressful times. As husbands, we are to provide for our wives' needs as adequately as possible, to keep them free from worry and cares. God told Adam to protect the garden, and he didn't do it very well. God wants us to do a better job than Adam did. He has given us someone to protect, to take care of. We have to protect our wives from the things that unduly concern them. Not hide it from them, but protect them, and that can take some doing!

A lot of times it is our own actions which cause our wives great dismay. Our lack of understanding or tenderness, our scorn for what interests her, our ignorance of women's needs, our unfaithfulness, whether in thought or deed, all cause great distress to them.

Shock Absorbers

One man describes the husband's role as that of a shock absorber. Just as Jesus smooths out the bumps for us, making the high places lower, and the low places higher, smoothing out the road we travel on, we are to do the same for our wives. It is downright uncomfortable to ride in a car that has no shock absorbers. There is no protection from the road's imperfections, nothing to absorb the harshness of pitted concrete or bumpy gravel. We are to be like a good set of shocks on the road of life for our wives. They need us to level things out, keep things smooth, to remain steady in tough times, to really care when they are upset and concerned. Many times just understanding how they feel, expressing that we do care makes all the difference in the world to them.

Jesus said He would never leave us nor forsake us, that He is the same, yesterday, today and forever. (Heb. 13:5,8.)

We know we can trust Him to be true to us on our good days, as well as the upsetting ones. Our wives need to know that we will be the same. They need to know at their emotional level we will always be there; we will not abandon them spiritually, mentally, emotionally, or physically, regardless of the circumstances.

Many times we think of abandonment as strictly something physical. We think if we are there, that is all that is necessary. But we can't abandon them emotionally, we need to keep communications going back and forth. Women feel isolated and alone when they are not hearing from us. It is important to share with her from your heart, letting her be a part of your life, too.

There are some pretty interesting truths in Ephesians 5:28-29.

> **So ought men to love their wives as their own bodies. He that loveth his wife, loveth himself. For no man ever yet hated his own flesh; but nourisheth and cherisheth it, even as the Lord the church.**

Essentially, those verses say you should respond to your wife the way you love and take care of yourself. How many times are you upset with yourself over some stupid thing you have done and, in turn, you take it out on your wife. Jesus also told us to love our neighbor as ourselves. That means we are definitely supposed to love ourselves or our neighbors in trouble! Love is forgiving and kind; love holds no ought against another; love doesn't even notice it has been wronged. Love is patient, long-suffering, and never fails.

In other words we are to be loving with ourselves as well as our wives. Love cherishes and nourishes, encourages, and builds up, supports and strengthens.

When my physical body is hurting, I want to do whatever I can to stop that pain. When it is hungry I feed it, when it is cold I clothe it, when it is dirty I bathe it, when it is sleepy I put it to bed. I give it as much loving care as I possibly can, and that is exactly what we are to do with our wives. We are to be like Jesus in every possible way when it comes to our wives. They are specially handcrafted creatures, delicately made to be our alter-ego, our other half. When we look into their eyes we are not just to see a reflection of ourselves, but of Jesus. He is in them and us.

Is He showing through, in you?

8
You've Found A Good Thing!

Have you ever received a gift that had great value to you? Because it meant so much to you, you probably displayed it proudly, cared for it lovingly, and appreciated it continually. You no doubt expressed great satisfaction and thanksgiving for that gift to the one who gave it to you. God has given you a priceless gift in your mate, and you ought to be thankful to the One Who gave her to you. You ought to display her with pride, taking wonderful care of her, for she is a gift from God.

One thing that often undoes this way of thinking is the terminology you have heard growing up. Without thinking you may still be giving voice to a carnal mentality today. When someone asks if that's your wife, you might say, "Oh, yeah, that's my old lady." What you have just said is, "She has no value to me." There is no proud displaying, no caring, no thanksgiving.

But we have reason to be thankful. Proverbs 18:22 states, **Whoso findeth a wife findeth a good thing, and obtaineth favour of the Lord.** Some women might resent being called a thing, until they realize what that verse means.

Notice she is called a "good thing." In the Hebrew, *good* refers to "agreeable, pleasant, and desirable; beautiful,... suitable;...becoming, virtuous; ...also applied to things prosperous and abundant; to happiness and joyfulness; to advantage and pleasure."[1] It means good in the greatest sense.

The word *thing* refers to "business," "advice,... commune (-ication), ...power, promise, provision, purpose...and song."[2]

And what else does she bring? Favor with the Lord! Because I have her, I have favor with the Lord! Hey, that makes her worth keeping right there, doesn't it? Oh, glory — a man who finds a wife finds a good thing! When you put the meaning of those two words together, you have something dynamic!

Because of the infiltration of the world's thinking, some have developed the mentality which says, "We'll just try it for a while, and if it doesn't work out, we'll forget it." That isn't covenant relationship. If there isn't a covenant, then you haven't found a good thing — you've just found somebody to shack up with! That's not right, and it's certainly not biblical! My daddy used to always tell my mama, "When you get to be forty, I'm going to trade you in on two twenty-year-olds." Sounded funny at the time, but it wasn't.

Favor With The Lord

Let's explore this aspect of obtaining favor with the Lord because we found a good thing in our wives. *To find favor* means "to be well pleased with, or to take delight in." It means "acceptance,...satisfaction; grace,...and good-will.[3] With that understanding, why would any man want to remain single? God places His utmost approval on marriage, delights in it, and extends His grace and goodwill to us because of our wives.

Sometimes men think they are a hot dog on a stick when the only reason they have any blessings is because of their wives. When I think of all the ways Pat has helped me, it boggles my mind. She has been involved in helping me with all four companies I presently own. She helped me in 1963 when we first started with Brother Hagin by setting up the office and following up on all the detail work. She set up the Harrison House office when I started the publishing company, and set up all the office procedures for Faith Christian Fellowship International when it was started.

I know men who don't want their wives knowing anything about their business involvement, but I have news for them. They need what their wives have. They may not be business oriented, but women have instincts and abilities to see things differently than men, to see another perspective. That is all part of her being a virtuous woman. She can help you in your personal business and in the job situation if you would just allow her. My wife and I are one. She has *a right* to say anything she wants to about my life. She is not butting in on my territory — we are one, and I need her input.

Just as the Father, Son and Holy Spirit are one, so you and your wife are one. You and she are with God, so the three of you are a triune being; therefore, she has a right and the privilege to function as God has created her to function. Don't tell her to mind her own business — *you are her business!* Let her do her job and help you. **Neither was the man created for the woman; but the woman for the man** (1 Cor. 11:9). He specifically made our wives for us, because we would have need of her as a helpmeet, not just because she is good looking or a good housekeeper. She is a good thing, to bring favor and goodness into our lives. The man who ignores this is a fool and will miss many of the benefits God has for him in marriage.

Proverbs 31:10-12 describes the virtuous woman.

Who can find a virtuous woman? for her price is far above rubies. The heart of her husband doth safely trust in her, so he shall have no need of spoil. She will do him good and not evil all the days of her life.

The word *virtuous* as used here refers to strength. It means "might," "strong," "able," "riches," "substance," "valour"⁴— of good quality, integrity. Who can put a price tag on this kind of blessing? His heart can safely trust in her. A man doesn't need to look elsewhere when he has a wife like her.

Did you notice that phrase about safely trusting in her? Truth must prevail between you two before friendship can come. Friends tell the truth to one another and from that truth, they learn to trust one another. What it is saying is if you can't trust your wife, she is not a good friend. It all begins with truth; truth brings trust which brings liberty, freedom.

Trust will stop the roving eyes. The lust of the eye can be a problem for you, but if you have a wife you can safely trust in, then that helps you to quit eyeballing everything else.

I know there is an old saying about men always looking, but there is a definite danger in eyeballing. Pretty soon the lust of the eye leads to other things: thoughts lead to imaginations, which become strongholds.

See, with that first thought comes a second, "Boy, look at that shape. I bet she's really hot in bed." Then you start to imagine how you could get her in bed. And if you imagine that long enough, it becomes a stronghold. Why is it a stronghold? Because you have submitted your will to it, you have thought "I'm going to get her in the rack!"

If you have built a trusting relationship with your wife, it will keep you on the right track. You will trust her and stop looking around at other women. She is your priceless gift from God, someone to be treasured and adored.

The Lesson Of Interdependence

I remember a time when I wanted to abandon my ministry. I just didn't think I could go on in the ministry any longer. We have all had times like that, when we were up to our armpits in alligators and just wanted out of the whole swamp. Our emotions overwhelm us. This particular time I told Pat I simply wanted to quit and move away where nobody would know us. Pat clearly and emphatically reminded me of all that God had promised. She strengthened my heart as she said, "I love you, Buddy, but we are not quitting the ministry God has called us to." That is so valuable!

I needed her strength in my time of weakness and, I don't mind telling you, I don't know where I would be today if she had not spoken so wisely! She was able to hang on when I wanted to let go. I can safely trust in her to obey God and always have my best interest at heart. It is just as hard on her, but she is thinking about me! That gives peace and confidence to a man!

Just as Pat is a strength to me, there are many times when I become strength for her. Husband and wife should be interdependent. We both have strengths and weaknesses. Her strengths are usually my weaknesses, and my strong areas fill in where she is weaker. Together, we become a balanced partnership. See how smart God is?

When we are born into the earth, we are dependent. A baby has to be fed, clothed, cared for. Babies are totally dependent upon others for getting their needs met. We immediately teach them to become independent, to be able to do for themselves. We are teaching them stewardship all along as well, of their bodies, their lives. The whole idea is to become independent, so they can brush their own teeth, bathe themselves, dress themselves, tie their own shoes, or whatever needs doing. Becoming independent sets up the third phase of life, which is interdependence. We can't be good at interdependence until we have first been good at independence. With interdependence we learn to submit our wills to another. We know we can make it on our own if we have to, but God wants us at a place where we have become interdependent.

As free moral agents we can make our own decisions, do our own thing, but He wants us to be interdependent with Him. You can live on this earth without God, but you will do a whole lot better with Him. If there is trust between you and God, you are relying on Him, but He is also relying on you. He is the Head, but we are the Body. You are supposed to be doing the work, with the Head speaking to you. You are a laborer together with God. If that is the case between God and man, shouldn't it be the same between husband and wife? You have given up your independence to become interdependent. That means there must be trust, reliance, a working together. This is what God is interested in. Sure you can make it by yourself, but there will be some things you will miss. Your strengths and weaknesses come together so we can produce things God wants and receive the blessings of God His way.

The Power Of Knowledge

It is vitally important to recognize and remember the differences between man and woman, which are a result of our creation. Men were squeezed together, so we have a tendency to be rather crude, rougher. But women were highly, skillfully handcrafted. They are more tender, more refined, more delicate in many ways.

Comparing men and women is like comparing pick-up trucks and foreign sports cars. A pick-up truck requires very little to run well. About all you have to do is keep gas and oil in it, tune it up occasionally, and it continues to function. But foreign sports cars have an entirely different nature. They are finely tuned machines that need constant attention and expert care to keep them running well. Specific tools are often needed to adjust these cars. The mechanic must understand that engine and fuss with it regularly to get it to purr like a kitten! That is how women are. They need more fussing, more attention than most of us guys. Give us some basic fundamentals and we can truck right on, but women they must be finely tuned to run well. Billy Crystal wisecracked one time that "Wives need a *reason* for having sex; men just need a place." The joke is funny because there is a lot of truth in that remark, isn't there? The difference is in the vehicle! We are made different from women!

Understanding and patience are important tools in keeping our wives "running well." Tender, loving words keep her engine running smoothly. Appreciation and compliance are like new spark plugs to that sports car. Respect and consideration keep her tuned just right. Observe the caution lights and adjust where necessary and she will purr like a kitten.

God addresses this need and requirement of husbands in 1 Peter 3:7:

> **Likewise ye husbands, dwell with them according to knowledge, give honor unto the wife, as unto the weaker vessel, and as being heirs together of the grace of life; that your prayers be not hindered.**

A lot of husbands don't have much knowledge about women — they don't understand how they think, or their make-up. But the Word cautions us here: if we don't treat our wives right, our prayers are affected! I don't know about you, but that catches my attention!

It is a command from the Word of God for us to dwell with our wives according to knowledge. Just as it takes knowledge to run a sports car, it takes knowledge to live with a woman! The prophet Hosea said, **My people are destroyed for lack of knowledge** (Hos. 4:6). Sometimes, when we don't know something, we need to study up on the subject. We husbands need to study our wives — find out what makes them tick and what motivates them. I will guarantee you, if you see that she is taken care of, she will take care of you!

A Woman's Place

In my life I have not always been the husband I should have been. In many instances, it was because I had the wrong examples and beliefs presented to me as a young boy. I was raised to believe a woman's place is in the home. You know, keep her barefoot and pregnant and she will be happy. When I started having difficulties and troubles, thank God I had a good father-in-law. He sat me down, talked to me and straightened out my thinking. He was forthright and practical, even talked to me about treating Pat right sexually, how to handle her.

He had an interest in telling me the truth in order to bring forth God's best for his daughter, but he also knew her and what she needed as a woman. He knew what was profitable for his daughter as a woman; he loved her, and I still appreciate all the truths he taught me. He had knowledge about women that I knew nothing of — he had truth from God's Word when all I had was carnal thinking and experience.

While women have many strengths, sometimes the sensitivity and emotional make-up of a woman can make her seem weaker. Notice I said seem that way. They seem more vulnerable and easily hurt. But often their ability to handle stress goes far beyond ours. We are to honor them for their sensitivity, not belittle them for it. Sir, your wife is your joint-heir of the grace of life with you! If she is diminished, so are you.

God doesn't observe gender in spiritual matters in the church. But in the home it is different. Husbands and wives have different functions in the home than in the church. When men fail to recognize their own inabilities, or limitations — when they are not always as sensitive to the promptings of the Holy Spirit as their wives are — they need and ought to have her by their side.

Women have many attributes similar to those of the Holy Ghost. They are often wonderful comforters, called alongside their husbands, just as the Holy Ghost is to the believer. They stand by us when we need it the most. They teach and direct our children and make powerful intercessors. They are strengtheners in our homes and churches, bringing unique beauty to our lives.

Pat has always been a tremendous asset to me in the ministry. We have a unique ministry together of flowing tongues and interpretation. There is often a physical demonstration to go along with what is being said. A lot of times I won't even look at her while she is giving the utterance in tongues. I will just close my eyes and shut her out. Later people will tell me that I displayed the same mannerisms and facial expressions when I have interpreted the tongues as she did when she gave the message. Not always, but often. A demonstration like that shows the uniqueness of God and how husband and wife can flow together. You see, *it is done by the Holy Spirit*, to bring forth that fullness, that beauty of what God desires all of us to have in our relationship.

Spiritual Equals — Different Graces and Gifts

Men and women are spiritual equals, yet with different graces and gifts to complement one another. There is no place for competition when we recognize and appreciate these truths. We are designed to have completion with one another, not competition against each other!

One of the most common ways this dynamic expresses itself is in the couple where one spouse is a broad conceptual thinker and the other is a precise detail oriented thinker. Another is the couple where one partner is highly emotional and the other is quite reserved. I am sure you can think of more examples because it seems nearly every couple is a mixture of opposites in one or more ways. This is on purpose! It is God's design to fulfill us. We become more than the sum of our two selves, we become one flesh.

The problem comes when we view our partners as our competitors, and not as our completers. Another wrong view we sometimes have is in relating to our spouse as though they were a child, constantly correcting and managing their life (most of the time just so we can feel better about ourselves) until they withdraw the intimacy we want so much.

A third wrong view is to regard your wife as a millstone, someone who constantly sucks emotional energy from you or makes demands upon you. Men, when you see that behavior in your wife, you are looking at a woman who is being shortchanged in the security department — by *you*. Ouch!

Understand, God made man the initiator. So start something! Pray! Make a change. Take the situation to God and ask how *you* can adjust things and yourself in order to give her the emotional support she needs to feel secure. I promise you, if she feels secure she will blossom right in front of you.

The fundamental lesson to be learned here is to begin to see your wife's differences from you as additional strengths you can rely on and not as contrary opinions or behaviors that threaten you or your position. If you feel threatened by your wife's opposite nature, then it is time to examine your own security base.

Are you looking to her to make you feel good about yourself so that you can then feel secure? Wrong. She didn't establish you as her head, God did! I know how important it is to look good in your wife's eyes, but if you focus on how you look in God's eyes then you will have no trouble with how you look to her. The stronger and closer your walk with the Lord becomes, the more secure she will feel.

I want to help you understand how crazy things can get when a husband starts backing off from the things of God (eventually he will run from them). Let me share an episode of mine which took place quite a few years ago when I did a bit of running myself. My attitude was all fouled up, as I wrote about earlier, and our marriage was really suffering.

Things got so bad that I took off from Pat and the kids. I had been raised in Houston and still had connections, so I thought I could find work there. I was fed up with everything, and blamed Pat and the kids, and anybody else I could think of. I was holding nightly pity parties. Brother Hagin happened to be in the area for a meeting, so I went to see him.

I walked into the trailer where he lived while on the road, and found him shaving. He took one look at me and said, "You know you've been running from God, don't you?" "Yeah," I said, "I know I'm running, and when I ain't running, I'm gonna be walking, and when I ain't walking, I'm gonna be crawling, and when I ain't crawling, I'm gonna be scratching." I was a spiritual mess, but until he addressed the issue squarely I was blaming everybody else and avoiding the truth.

I realized during that whole time I had been ranting and raving at Pat, hollering and accusing her of ugly things, that she had just sat there quietly. First Peter 3:1-4 speaks of a woman's meek and quiet spirit and how her chaste manner of living will draw her husband to follow God's Word. It was Pat's quiet spirit and her pure manner of living that had such a great effect on me. Because her way of life was such a contrast to mine, I finally saw how wrong I had been. Within three weeks I was back in fellowship with God, had gotten a job and was back with my family — all because of her grace in that situation.

Proverbs 12:4 states, **A virtuous woman is a crown to her husband.** The word *crown* has several connotations. It means "to encircle" or "compass" about.[5] It implies protection from attack while encompassing. That is what our wives do when they pray for us. They encircle us with support and strength through prayer. I praise God for a praying wife.

The dictionary defines *crown* as "something that imparts splendor, honor, or finish: culmination...to bring to a successful conclusion."[6] This kind of wife helps her husband reach his greatest potential, achieve his greatest heights. I know personally I would not be where I am today if it were not for my wife's influence.

There is an old saying in the world, "Behind every successful man there is a good woman." I believe this is truth and the way God intended it all along. According to 1 Corinthians 11:7, **Woman is the glory of the man.** Glory brings splendor and honor to something. Have you ever noticed how good a man looks when he has a great looking woman by his side? She is designed to bring him esteem, just by being with him. I have had people tell me I look better when Pat is with me. That is because we are one flesh, and she brings splendor where I am lacking. A good wife really is a good thing! Pat is a blessing from God given to me to cherish. When God said it wasn't a good thing for man to be alone, He created the finest thing a man could ever have: a helpmeet to bring completion, assistance, benefits, glory and favor.

She is a good thing!

9
Leaving So You Can Cleave!

After God created Eve for Adam He gave a command: **Therefore shall a man leave his father and his mother, and shall cleave unto his wife: and they shall be one flesh** (Gen. 2:24). It is interesting that this command was given before there were any parents on the earth. God must have foreseen the problems some people would have leaving their parents when they were married. Oftentimes the parents have just as much trouble letting go of their offspring.

A godly parent will, as a part of their parenting responsibilities, prepare their children for the various stages of adulthood and cut those proverbial apron strings at the right time. But just as young birds don't like being pushed out of the nest even when they are ready to fly, some young people resist leaving the parental family even when it is obviously time to do so. In fact, I have known men and women who still have an unhealthy attachment to their parents when they themselves are ready to be grandparents.

Leaving your father and mother is more than physically moving out of their home. It is leaving the comfort zone of their nurture and protection. It is taking full control and full responsibility for your own decisions and the direction of your life, and Dad and Mom assume an advisory position rather than a directive one. Spiritually, you leave their household and establish your own which includes your wife and any family you have in the future. Certainly you never stop loving, respecting and honoring your parents; however, they should no longer have the same position and priority in your life they once had.

God made it clear that in order to cleave one must first leave. If a man is continually running back to his parents instead of preferring his wife, he hasn't really left. If he is continually comparing his wife to his mother, he hasn't really left. If he cannot make decisions with his mate unless he has parental approval, he hasn't left. If he runs to Mama every time he and his wife disagree, he hasn't really left.

The reverse problem, the wife continually running to her parents for support and comfort, is equally wrong. But, before you throw the entire blame on her, ask yourself if you have been the type of husband to whom she can safely entrust herself.

Women are very security minded. One reason women never really leave their parents is because they aren't secure in their husband's love. They need to feel protected by their husbands in all areas of life. If they don't get it from you, they will look elsewhere. If Mama and Daddy have always been there for her, that is where she will run! If her parents have always had a listening ear, and you don't, guess who she will be talking to? If you don't show her affection and they do, she will get it from them or somebody else!

Cutting The Cord

Shortly after our daughter Cookie married her husband, Fred, they moved to South Africa to assist in a ministry. I hadn't realized just how close the ties were between Cookie and me. She was used to coming to me with all her problems. She used to sit on my lap and hug me even as a young woman. So when she married, we would get these long distance calls from a frustrated Fred on the other end. He would say, "Dad, you gotta talk to Cookie." What was happening was every time Fred made a decision she would say, "That's not the way my Dad did it!" and they would end up arguing. Fred didn't know what to do with her. I had to tell her over and over, "Cookie, he's your husband. He's a godly man, and you need to listen to him!"

It took some time, but she finally learned. You see, at that point, if we had encouraged her to run to us with her troubles, which would make us feel needed, we would have started a cycle that would have had the ability to break their marriage. As parents we had to untie those apron strings and insist they work together as a team. We had to teach Cookie not to prefer our advice over Fred's all the time.

Thank God Pat never went to her folks with our troubles. I figure they had a hard enough time staying in faith over me as her husband anyway. And whenever I went to Brother Hagin for advice, he gave me God's Word on the subject along with common sense and good practical tips. He knew I didn't have a father who taught me right in marriage matters, so he was patient and kind, but always honest and forthright with me. I knew I could trust his counsel, and he wouldn't try to manipulate me!

Manipulation is a form of control that can be devious and deadly to a marriage. Some parents haven't learned how to let go of their adult children. They can exert control in subtle ways the offspring may be accustomed to, so the child fails to recognize them. These traits are handed down from generation to generation and, therefore, seem normal to family members. Guilt and condemnation are heaped on those who attempt to loose themselves from the controlling grip. Accusations such as "you don't love me anymore" or "after all I've done for you all these years..." are common.

It takes a strong man or woman to stand up to parental control, but it must be done to secure a good marriage. God's Word is clear on this issue. He set the pattern in the garden. The two are to cleave together and become one flesh. Once married, a couple is a new family unit, even before children arrive.

Marriage is a precious, holy institution in God's sight. It is your responsibility to keep it that way in your own home by keeping your priorities in order.

Your first priority is your personal relationship with God. Next is your own well-being, spirit, soul and body. If you fail to take care of yourself, you are no good to anyone else. Your next priority — before the kids, before work, before ministry, and before your parents — is your wife.

If your parents refuse to acknowledge your marital priority, you may have to have a loving but firm talk with them. If they have been controlling, you will have to take authority over this in prayer before speaking to them. Sometimes parental patterns have been established for a long time so you must remain steadfast and diligent to stick to your convictions.

Trust God to move on your behalf and show you creative ways to continue your stand. The trick here is not to push them away, but to show them you two are more than capable of handling your own life together. Help them understand that while you might not do everything the way they would, you can manage to handle things to your own satisfaction. Reassure them their counsel is still valuable to you, and that you would like to be able to still call on their wisdom and experience when you feel you need it.

Correction in your own thinking and habits is necessary to walk free from unhealthy behavior. If you have been accustomed to running to your parents instead of God every time you are in trouble or have a problem, repent and ask the Holy Spirit to help you correct your attitudes and actions. Renew your mind to God's promises and acknowledge that He is Lord over your life in all areas. Pray the prayer of agreement with your wife regarding family decisions and difficult circumstances, and expect God to move on your behalf.

What A Catch!

While leaving parents may be difficult, cleaving to your wife should bring ultimate joy and satisfaction. The word *cleave* means "to cling or adhere...to catch by pursuit"[1]; in other words, to never stop chasing. I like that!

I remember years ago I was always trying to find ways to get my wife into bed. Then I would scold myself for being so carnal and unspiritual. So, in an attempt to be more spiritual, I would start praying, but soon I found myself praying for ways to get her into bed. Then I read Genesis 2:24 and realized I was lining up with God's Word all along! In my chasing Pat around the house I was cleaving! I was being scriptural! What relief that brought to my heart!

Yes, it was God who placed "the urge to merge" within us. He created the sexual act to be a beautiful time of intimacy and oneness for both partners. Unfortunately, it isn't that way in every marriage.

In Genesis 18:12 after Sarah hears she is to bring forth their promised heir, she replied, **After I am waxed old shall I have pleasure, my Lord being old also?** Evidently Sarah viewed intercourse as pleasant, not just her wifely duty, and Abraham must have known how to bring his wife pleasure. So many men selfishly satisfy their own sexual needs without regard to their wife's needs. As men, we must realize our important role in bringing sexual pleasure to our wives.

As men we know how easy it is to simply fulfill the physical without experiencing any intimacy at all; but to a woman, intimacy is more than intercourse. Your wife needs a sense of closeness and sharing that goes well beyond the act. She desires relationship with you that includes conversations of the heart. She needs affirmations of your affection and devotion towards her. She needs to know she is number one in your heart after the Lord.

For a woman to totally release herself into a man's arms, there must be trust and commitment. You see, Jesus said He would never leave us nor forsake us. When we know He is true to His Word, we can trust our lives entirely to Him. There is safety and assurance there. We know no matter what, He will always love us. We can relax in His loving arms and yield ourselves to Him.

Likewise, for a woman to yield herself sexually this same kind of trust is essential. If there is no trust, she will have difficulty achieving total fulfillment. During the time of a woman's arousal, just before she is to have an orgasm, she experiences a lack of control. Her body has responded in such a manner that she will soon be unable to stop. But if she cannot totally trust herself with a man, unconsciously she won't allow herself to reach that point.

For some women, not trusting men in general is the problem. Incest, rape and sexual molestation in the past can greatly hinder women from freely enjoying intercourse. And many mothers have passed on their disrespect and distrust towards men to their daughters. Television hasn't been much help either. Not only are the vast majority of men and women on the tube poor role models for biblically based relationships, but the quick and easy availability of television viewing is a form of anesthesia to romance. It is a lot easier to plop down in the chair and click on the TV with a remote, than it is to spend the time developing your relationship with your wife.

The Art of Romance

In addition, an essential element for a woman's sexual fulfillment is romance! Remember, she is usually more emotional than you are and, therefore, needs emotional preparation. A man can just take one look at her scantily dressed body and he is ready! That is because he is aroused by sight, but she is aroused by feelings and touches.

If the only time you are the least bit romantic is when you want her sexually, she won't always want to respond to your passes. How would you feel if Jesus only told you He loved you when He wanted something? Did you ever notice that He is continually loving us and wooing us so that we just can't resist responding to Him? Even when we aren't too sweet and loving, He is always patient and kind towards us. Remember, He is our example, men!

Think back to those days before marriage, when you and your wife were dating. How did you treat her then? You probably did whatever you could to impress her in the romance department. You made special efforts to look, smell and act your best. You sent her flowers, took her to romantic places, bought special gifts for no reason other than you loved her. You whispered sweet words in her ear as you held her closely, and promised her the moon if she asked for it! Nothing was too good for your girl!

Your wife fell in love with the man who continually romanced her, who charmed her until she finally married him. Now true love goes beyond romance, but since we are to continue cleaving unto our wives, we must realize that it is those same little things we did to attract her before marriage that will keep the flame burning thirty years later. How about learning some new things as well? Christian bookstores have several books on how to date your wife.

Most men crave what they do not yet possess. God created us to be conquerors so we would concentrate all our energies and efforts on conquering what we desire to possess. We always want better jobs, greater ministries, finer cars, bigger boats, etc. Once a man obtains his desired goal, he will then focus all his energies and abilities on something else, something greater, a new conquest.

Now consider how this affects a man's marriage. He expends any amount of creativity and effort needed to get his woman to the altar. Once he has married her, she is conquered! So then he focuses all his energy and abilities on pursuing other goals — possibly his career. Without realizing it, pursuing his wife no longer takes precedence. Soon, if he is not careful, he takes his wife's presence for granted — she is always there and she knows he loves her, doesn't she? After all, he provides for her; he comes home faithfully every evening. He thinks that should satisfy her, but it usually isn't enough.

Many women, who have dreamed of their wedding day since they were little girls, believe life for them begins at the altar! Great expectations of an enduring relationship that surpasses anything Hollywood could ever produce on screen usually reside in the heart of a starry-eyed bride. She has envisioned this wonderful knight in shining armor who would sweep her off her feet, carrying her into Marriage Wonderland! During the dating process, she became used to her knight's romantic actions, expecting them to last forever, not just until the honeymoon is over. She believed the way you were toward her was the real you, the way you really felt about her, and a part of the reality of your relationship. Is it any wonder, then, that women feel cheated or conned when romance ends after the marriage?

In case you are thinking it is just too much trouble to continue in the romantic vein, or that it is something Hollywood dreamed up and has no place in reality, let's take a look at some Scriptures. Proverbs 5:18-19 says:

> **Let thy fountain be blessed: and rejoice with the wife of thy youth. Let her be as the loving hind and pleasant roe; let her breasts satisfy thee at all times; and be thou ravished always with her love.**

The NIV translates that last part: **...may you ever be captivated by her love.** Men, we are to be great lovers of our wives, forever! The ancient Jewish writing instructed husbands to read the Song of Solomon to their wives on the Sabbath Eve and partake of sexual relations and recreation! Sounds like a great way to spend Sunday afternoon to me.

The Wisdom of Solomon

The Song of Solomon is a wonderful love story, full of romance and lovemaking. In chapter one, verse 13, the woman compares her man to a bundle of myrrh, saying, **...he shall lie all night betwixt my breasts.** Myrrh was used in making perfumes. He must have smelled good enough for her to want his body close to her the entire night. In chapter two he sets the stage for romance by taking her out to dinner: **He brought me to the banqueting house, and his banner over me was love** (2:4). No wonder it was recommended reading.

The book goes on to describe their embraces, their desires towards one another, foreplay details and even their bedroom decor. It is full of affectionate phrases of their love. Chapter 5 verse 16 states, **His mouth is most sweet: yea, he is altogether lovely. This is my beloved, and this is my friend, O daughters of Jerusalem** (5:16). The term *sweet* means "tender speech."[2] He spoke sweetly to her of his love. And did you notice she called him her friend as well. They had a good, trusting relationship, shared intimacies with each other, loved being together and joining together in that love.

In the Song of Solomon it is obvious that both the woman and man enjoyed their sexual activities. He knew how to arouse her and she responded to his advances eagerly. Foreplay prepared her to yield herself to him completely. Not only is foreplay essential for a woman to be fully aroused, but it also prepares her body to receive a man without pain. As lubricants are secreted naturally, her vaginal muscles are expanding and tightening. When a woman's body is fully ready, intercourse is more pleasurable for both parties.

Foreplay should be a time of creative expressions of your love through words, caresses and kissing. Because women peak much slower than men, lovemaking can be frustrating unless we realize that God created our bodies differently from animals' bodies, which have sex simply to procreate. For humans, sex is intended to be a beautiful time of intimacy and sharing. Patience on our part, men, will bring greater rewards for both parties because the longer the foreplay, the greater the climax!

I have learned that in my relationship with Pat if I will prefer her sexually, seeing that her needs are met first, mine will always be satisfied.

My father-in-law helped me in this area! He spoke frankly to me about satisfying a woman's needs in bed. I have heard so many women complain about their husbands, stating they have never experienced a climax in their lives. They remained frustrated because their husbands only care about satisfying their own needs, and when that was done, the loving was over. That is selfish gratification and not true fulfillment for either partner, let alone an act of becoming one flesh!

If you love and care for your wife, you will understand that a woman's make-up and nature begins with her emotions and her will — a man just sets his will. He gets the facts and a lot of times, the fact is, he wants to make love. His emotions come in somewhere along the way.

But for a woman, her whole thing begins with her emotions. That is why it is so important to take care of your wife and prefer her at this moment. If you will purpose in your lovemaking to do everything you can to achieve *her* highest point of satisfaction, I guarantee you she will become a better lover for you as well.

If you are doing it right, your wife can reach multiple climaxes, in foreplay and when you come together. You will have brought her into that glorious moment of total ecstasy for both of you. If you are willing to put aside your selfishness and say, "I want you taken care of first," you will become the best lover she could ever want.

We live in a society where everything is instant; where we are geared to doing things quickly. If we are not careful that approach can infiltrate our love life. Be willing to take the time with her, do whatever is necessary to build her to that point where your priority in lovemaking is seeing her needs fulfilled. It is all based on giving. Give and it shall be given unto you applies in the bedroom as much as in any other area of our lives.

On the practical side, be sure you have showered and shaved before making advances to your wife. And if you have ignored her all evening, watched TV while she put the kids to bed, did a load of laundry and cleaned up the kitchen, you may not be eagerly awaited in bed that night. If your hands are rough and your mannerisms crude, you won't be first on her hit parade either!

Unsettled differences between the two of you can also hinder sexual relationships for her. Because women are relationship oriented, if your relationship with her is out of whack, it will be very difficult for her to give herself to you with a whole heart. Also, the fear of an unplanned pregnancy will keep her from relaxing and yielding unless precautions are taken.

Many women battle feelings of shame and undesirability concerning their bodies. All their lives they have compared themselves to other females they have known. More than anything else in this area, women want to know that their beauty is more than enough to keep your interest. They want to be attractive in your eyes, as your opinion far outweighs anyone else's. Let her know how lovely she is to you, and do it regularly, creatively and frequently. And don't comment on other women's figures.

A Deeper Look

Let's look at a deeper level of understanding marriage and the sexual art. God created marriage to be a blood covenant, where both parties would give their all to one another. Blood covenants in the ancient world outside Israel usually involved blood letting because life was represented in the blood. Typically, the two parties entering into covenant would place a deliberate cut in their own hand or wrist and allow their blood to intermingle as a testimony to the commitment of their lives to one another.

In marriage, when husband and wife join together sexually, there is also a demonstration of the blood covenant which exists between them.

When a woman who is a virgin comes to the marriage bed, there is a breaking or penetrating of her hymen, generally causing a shedding of blood. With men, it is a little different. Scientists have discovered a man's semen has a microscopic trace of blood in it; therefore, each time he releases semen into his wife his life is represented in that union. In essence, he is renewing that covenant commitment he made with her on their wedding day. So then, lovemaking is not just for physical, sexual gratification, but it is a reenactment of the covenant as an expression of that union. Every time that semen enters her, it is reaffirming that the two of you are one flesh, that your life is hers and hers is yours.

It is the same covenant dynamic at work as when we have an intimate relationship with God, when we know him or have spiritual intercourse through worship and prayer with him, there is an exchange of life and love and strength.

So it is with man and wife. We become fused together spirit, soul and body. It is a holy time, a holy act, a time of sharing our most intimate part with one another, a time of complete satisfaction and total ecstasy, a consummation of our total beings intertwined with God's love!

Finally, it should be pointed out that a healthy, loving, intimate sexual relationship with your wife is one of the most powerful forms of spiritual warfare there is! Think about it for a moment. Let's put together a few things we already know about spiritual warfare and see how they are apply here. We know that the prayer of agreement is one of the most powerful forms of prayer for doing spiritual battle. Two believers cannot get into any closer agreement than that of being one flesh. Then too, we know that faith worketh by love and you can't get anymore in love with someone than you can your wife. So here we have the most powerful three elements — love, faith, and agreement — all working together at their maximum effectiveness at the same time. No wonder the Devil wants to destroy marriages.

Men, if only we could take hold of the awesome power we possess when we are operating in a covenant of love joined together in faith to pray the prayer of agreement. The church would never be the same!

10
Who's In Control?

Have you ever noticed that men who know almost nothing about the Bible can quote the verse, **Wives, submit yourselves unto your own husbands** (Eph. 5:22)? They just love to think they can exert their authority over a woman, as if that makes them somehow better! And what is worse, they use the Scripture like a club to emotionally batter the woman into something they call submission. The problem with this line of thinking is it simply isn't scriptural! If their conception of submission were correct it would make God a respecter of persons and we know He is not. Submission has nothing to do with power trips or dominance. No, submission is a matter of order, an order which God ordained.

God made man the head of his wife because man was created first. And woman was created for man. Each has their separate function and responsibilities. It is time to bury this macho man mentality of men barking orders around and dominating the home. God never gave anyone dominion over another person — only over the animals! When are we going to wake up to the truth, come in line with what the Word says, and be what we are supposed to be? Godly men lovingly leading, husbanding and protecting our wives.

In my book *Understanding Authority for Effective Leadership* I discuss levels of authority on the earth. It might help you to read it if you don't understand the man's God-given role as an effective leader.

I don't intend to repeat all that was written in that book, but one important truth does bear repetition! Authority and responsibility go hand in hand. Authority never exceeds responsibility; neither does it rightfully come without acceptance of responsibility. Therefore, you are responsible before God and accountable to Him regarding your headship in your home. You cannot expect your wife to be any more submitted to you than you are to the Lord.

Leading By Example

Now, let's take a look at Scriptures regarding headship and submission. First Corinthians 11:3 says: **But I would have you know, that the head of every man is Christ; and the head of the woman is the man; and the head of Christ is God.** (In the context of these verses, the word *man* refers to husband, *woman* to wife.[1])

Notice the first thing mentioned: Christ is our head! He has both authority and responsibility over us. In other words, we are not the ones in control. He is! That ought to help a man see things more clearly. It is not just what you want that counts — it is what He wants!

The word *head* does not mean that object sitting on your neck. In the Greek it means something from which you are a reflection. The moon is a reflection of the sun. The husband is to be a reflection of Christ in the home. The wife, then, is to be a reflection of her husband, who in turn is a reflection of Jesus. Paul prefaced these Scriptures by saying, **Be ye followers of me, even as I also am of Christ** (1 Cor. 11:1).

Just as Paul was urging his readers to follow his Christ-like example, we, as husbands, are urged to be that same kind of example to our wives and children. The question is what kind of an example are you? Does your wife see Jesus in your dealings with the family, or does she see selfishness? Does she see love and devotion or does she see dominance?

Does she see leadership or lethargy? The issue then for us men is not how well our wives are submitting to us, but how well we are leading them! I have studied a lot about leadership and found much confusion on the subject; but I have concluded there are certain qualities necessary for good leadership. Let's consider some of these in the light of your role as husband.

True spiritual leadership starts on the inside — knowing God and being submissive to His will. It is more important than what we do in life. So just because you may be a good provider does not mean you are a qualified leader. Being is more important than doing, and your doing must be spirit originated and controlled which begins by being in Him!

Now let's ask ourselves a few questions, do a checkup from the neck up. Have you ever broken yourself of a bad habit? To lead others you must be a master of yourself in Christ. If you can't manage yourself, no one else will want to follow you because they won't feel confident placing their trust in you.

Do you maintain control of yourself when things go wrong? Adversity and crisis often bring out irrational reactions rather than reasonable responses, as a result of having uncorrected bad habits. Just because a crisis comes shouldn't mean you go out of control. You exercise control when you choose the right response! Remember, anger is always a secondary response and normally based in fear. Be strong, not angry.

Are you an independent thinker or must you rely on others' opinions to make your decisions? Can your wife trust your decisions, knowing they are not selfish or self-centered, but rather what is best for the family? Weighing and judging others' opinions isn't wrong, but if the final decision rests with you, she needs to know it is the right one for all concerned and that she had the opportunity for input that was seriously considered. Not only that, if she is intimately acquainted with the process of decision making you use, and knows you are willing to submit all decisions to God, then she will have greater confidence in your leadership.

Can you readily secure the respect, cooperation and confidence of others? Does your family respect you as well as others who don't live with you? Can you administer discipline without resorting to a show of authority? True leadership is a quality of the spirit and requires no show of external force. I don't mean to give the impression that you shouldn't spank your children. Proverbs 13:24 states: **He that spareth his rod hateth his son: but he that loveth him chasteneth him betimes.** But if you have to stand over your children with a belt to get them to do their chores, you are a browbeater, not a leader!

Some people love authority because they love to flaunt it. I personally view leadership, whether in my home, in ministry or business, as a sacred, humbling thing. It is God-given, awesome and sometimes even scary!

Pull, Don't Push!

How many times have you walked up to the glass door of a business and pushed to open it, only to have the door slam up against the frame and give your shoulder a jolt? Then you take a closer look at the door and notice the "PULL" sign. I don't know about you, but right about then I feel plain dumb. You would think we would all look at the sign before we tried to open the door, and save ourselves a lot of embarrassment, but no, we just assume we know what to do and go on pushing instead of pulling.

It is the same when it comes to leading people, especially our families. Sometimes we just assume that the pushing approach, which works to some extent in the business world, is the proper approach at home. But a leader cannot push people; he must pull them. You pull them in, pull them up, pull them out, but you can't push them. Remember, we believers are sheep. Sheep do not herd real well. They must be led. I have found any time I tried to push Pat into anything, which I tried often back in my carnal days, it never worked. In fact, it usually back-fired on me! It isn't God's way; therefore, it won't accomplish His purposes.

Can you accept opposition to your viewpoint or decision without considering it a threat or a personal affront, and react accordingly? Just because your wife doesn't agree with your opinions doesn't mean she doesn't love you or respect you. We all think we are right at times, and anyone who opposes us just doesn't see it right. But how do you react, especially when the opposition is from your wife?

Sometimes it just boils down to being willing to be wrong and to admit it if you are. Learn to let it be OK if you miss dead center once in a while. Women instinctively trust and love a man who is not afraid to show his vulnerable side now and again. You see, she is smart enough to know you are going to make a wrong decision every so often, so if she never sees you goof she keeps waiting for the other shoe to drop. Fear builds up because she knows she is not seeing reality. Be real and you will be rewarded! This platform of honesty is key in maintaining the love walk with your wife.

Do you constantly need someone to stroke you or are you self-starter? Must you continually have another's approval or praise to function? Does she have to nag you or sweet-talk you to fix the plumbing?

Do you possess a strong, steadfast will in all three areas of your life — spirit, soul and body? I am not talking about being bull-headed, but about remaining steadfast and immovable. Willpower should be God's will working through our will, with our acceptance and acknowledgment that it is His power working in us! Our mind is the pivot point. If we, as men, can't control our wills, how can we expect our wives to control theirs? We are to lead them by example!

As a reflection of Jesus to our wives, we must look at His life as the example for us. He says He is the Good Shepherd. Psalm 23 describes the responsibilities of our Good Shepherd. If a husband will seek after the shepherd's heart, and lead his wife as a shepherd leads his flock, there would be fewer divorces in the land. Wives would never experience lack, for their husbands would provide peace, security and comfort for them. They would prosper in their homes, their souls would experience restoration when needed, righteousness would prevail, and even in dark times, there would be no reason to fear.

He would be with them, using the Word of God and his authority against all their enemies. He would continually fill their lives with good things. Goodness and mercy would be household qualities that lasted forever. A shepherd will willingly lay down his life for his sheep. Their needs come first, and he meets them!

You may think that is a tall order, even an impossible one, but I consider it an honor as well as a challenge to be a husband. I don't mind taking responsibility when I realize God never calls me to anything without equipping me with the abilities needed to accomplish the assignment. The Spirit of God showed Pat that *responsibility was simply our response to the ability of God within us.* God created us to be husbands, so we simply need to respond to that call and to the grace which is within us! After all, He created our wives, too, and He knows exactly what they need.

Walking Under Authority

Do you remember the Roman officer who approached Jesus on behalf of his servant who needed healing? He noted that Jesus was a man under authority, which was why He walked in authority. It is the same for us! We must walk *under* authority to really walk *in* authority!

When you submit yourself to the headship of Jesus and to doing things His way, He not only leads you from within, but He also leads your family through you so that all of you will be blessed. Remember, I made the point earlier that God was, and is, no respecter of persons? He set up the order of marriage so there would be a clear channel through which His blessing could flow. But that means submission should start with the husband! That's right! After all, if your wife is to follow your example, you had better be sure it is a submitted one. That, my friend, is where real authority starts!

Let me show you how key this concept is to being an effective, godly husband. One of our ministers was planning his wedding a few years ago, and he and his bride-to-be had decided on a certain date for their ceremony. About a month later this man was in prayer and the Lord told him to move the date forward three months. Startled, the man asked the Lord for a confirmation, which he received. He then discussed the matter with his fiancée who had been quite firm about the later date. After several minutes of give and take discussion in which he made sure she got to say everything she had to say, he told her he would take it up again with the Lord. He did, and got the same answer as before.

Their next discussion was much shorter. The man explained he had put the matter before the Lord, as he said he would, and had received the same answer as before: to move the wedding date forward three months. He also let her know he was aware of the extra burden the shorter time would place on her and all the changes in the plans that would have to be made. But, he felt that was the direction the Lord had given him, so therefore, he explained gently, even though they both preferred the later time, they would move the date up. She looked at him for a moment and then smiled. A major change was made with no strife at all because he was submitted to his Head and so was she.

Three months later the wedding went off without a problem. The flowers were free, the cake was donated, the honeymoon cottage was gratis, and the reception was paid for by a church member — all because they had been obedient. Then, the reason for the change in the wedding date manifested itself. A personal attack was launched by the enemy, but because this couple was now married, the Devil was left in the dust, defeated! Victory was theirs because the husband was submitted to his Head, Jesus, and his wife was submitted to hers, her husband.

Head Of The Home

One other thing concerning headship. While the husband is the head of his wife, he is not the head of the home. Now before you get bent out of shape on this, let's look at 1 Timothy 5:14. This was written concerning widows, but the principle applies to all women. **I will therefore that the younger women marry, bear children, guide the house....** The phrase *guide the house* means "to be the head of (i.e. rule) a family."[3] It means to be a household executive or administrator. Think about the virtuous woman in Proverbs 31. Wasn't she the household administrator? Didn't she run the household affairs and, as a result, her works were praised?

When it comes to our home, I certainly don't tell Pat what groceries to buy, or how to decorate the living room. She is well able to administrate our home in a competent manner, and I am grateful she does it. That is her department, her sphere of responsibility and authority, and I don't mess with it! While there are always some decisions we share, as a whole, that house is her baby! She often does things with me in mind, but it is hers to run.

Men who refuse to allow their wives to "guide the house" must recognize a vital truth: women are the very heart of a home. She sets the tone for the home so that the house should reflect her personality. In fact, one can tell a lot about a woman by seeing how she has decorated her home. Her unique style will show through. She is going to want to take good care of a home that reflects her personality, and she will enjoy being in it. But if you are telling her how to decorate it, and you are making all the decisions about it, and you are ruling the roost like a banty rooster, Mama ain't gonna be too happy! Isn't there an old saying, "If Mama ain't happy, ain't nobody happy!" And, it is contrary to the way God designed it!

So where does a wife's submission fit into all of this? We have already understood that the husband should rightfully set the example by submitting unto Christ, but often he learns true submission from a godly wife! God created her to be submissive as a helpmeet; she has special graces in this area. Let's look at Biblical submission a bit more.

> **Submitting yourselves one to another in the fear of God. Wives, submit yourselves unto your own husbands, as unto the Lord. For the husband is the head of the wife, even as Christ is the head of the church: and he is the savior of the body. Therefore as the church is subject unto Christ, so let the wives be to their own husbands in everything.**
>
> **Ephesians 5:21-24**

Notice mutual submission out of reverence for God is mentioned first. Next, wives are told to submit themselves unto their *own* husbands, not somebody else's, as unto the Lord. Again, this should be done in reverence for God, but also as unto the Lord, or in the same way she submits unto Him.

We all know that God never asks her to do anything against His Word, or His will, nor against her conscience. Therefore, if you are to be her head as Christ is the Head of the church, and she is to submit unto you as she does unto Him, you must be sure you are not asking her to violate herself in any of those areas. Headship in the home is relational while headship in the Church is spiritual. You aren't your wife's spiritual head, Christ is. She is accountable to Him regarding her personal prayer and Bible study, church attendance, etc.

Even as the head of the relationship, we sometimes think of submission in military or worldly terms. In our carnal minds, the old "Me BOSS, you SLAVE" mentality looms big if we don't understand true Biblical submission.

The strength of the word *submit* as used in Ephesians 5:21 does not refer to obedient actions, but rather to adapting.[4] Therefore, it is an *attitude of the heart* that God commands, not a military chain of command as many have supposed.

Actions can appear right when the attitude is all wrong. They may look submissive, but that doesn't mean they are! God judges the intent of our hearts and He knows the difference whether or not those around us do. Remember, he made man and woman to see eye to eye. He created woman to stand beside her man, not beneath him, nor behind him. He made her to aid and surround him and to support him. As a helpmeet she has been graced with the ability to adapt. Look back to the original plan God intended for marriage and get the right perspective. God wants unity, a husband and wife working and praying together with one mind and one heart concerning relationship issues.

You see, when we operate in God's order it becomes apparent we are not complete without one another. I am not complete without Pat, and she is not complete without me. Man was not made for the woman, but woman for the man, and yet we balance one another in our completion of each other. That is God's order of things, as it was in the beginning. If the order is right, then it will work right. It is the same in our marriage.

Usually when a home is out of order it is pretty obvious. Either we see a macho man mentality or a mealy mouthed character who won't stand up and be a man. In the latter case, the woman has to stand up and do what is right because her husband won't do it. We are pretty quick to blame the woman, when all along it is the man who is to blame. He is out of order and therefore so is the marriage.

Right order in a marriage produces a powerful unit. We as men must accept our wives' role as helpmeet to keep that order right, that marriage powerful. I used to get irritated with Pat when she was only trying to help me. I didn't see it as help. I saw it as fault-finding. For example, we would be getting ready for a service, when she would say "You've got a string hanging on the back of your britches." I would think, "Well, so what...I want to feel a little stringy today." Or I would put on my shirt and tie, and comb my hair again, before putting my sports jacket on. She would start brushing hair off my back, and I would bark, "Get your hands off me, woman!" Here she was trying to surround me with aid and assistance, but because of my perspective, I couldn't receive it. In turn, that wouldn't allow her to function the way she is called to function. Things were out of order because of my lack of knowledge and understanding about my need for her help.

See, just because God made us the head, doesn't mean we don't need help. What good is a head without the rest of the body? It is incomplete! He made us a helpmeet because we need help!

So to keep things in order, I must remember my function and authority *and hers*. Neither one of us is greater or more important; we are both simply following orders.

Jesus was talking with His disciples one time about who would be the greatest among them. They were concerned about position, but Jesus went to the heart of the matter. First of all, He noted that the Gentiles (or the world) exercised dominion and authority over those who were under them — the greater they were in position, the greater dominion they exhibited. But, He said:

> ...it shall not be so among you: but whosoever will be great among you, let him be your minister [bond-slave]:...Even as the Son of man came not to be ministered unto, but to minister, and to give his life a ransom for many.
>
> Matthew 20:26-28

Jesus not only described true greatness in God's kingdom as servanthood, but He demonstrated it in His own life and death. He served those around Him lovingly and humbly, even going as far as performing a servant's task: washing His disciples' dirty feet. He then laid down His life for them — and us — willingly and lovingly, never once demanding that others submit to His authority, never treating them as beneath Himself. Jesus used His authority to subdue demonic forces. The people who followed Him did so out of hearts of love and thanksgiving, not obligation.

When a husband treats his wife as Christ does the Church, she longs to lovingly submit herself to him. When he forgets trying to be the head honcho and treats her with respect and consideration, recognizing her place beside him and his need for her, she will go out of her way to adapt to him and please him.

If we are doing it right in our home, guys, control won't even be an issue because the only One in control will be the Holy Spirit. When differences arise about finances, or disciplining the children, or vacation plans, or whatever, the first approach you take should be one of praying together. God is your source and united prayer settles an issue as nothing else can.

Decisions, Decisions, Decisions

The Bible says when two agree together, that is, harmonize together as an orchestra would,[5] in prayer, asking according to God's will, it shall be done for them in heaven. (Matt. 18:19; 1 John 5:14.) Agreement means you have already talked it out before you pray, agreeing in your hearts and minds to the same thing. If it is an issue you don't agree on, find out what you *can* come into agreement on, and work from there. If, after prayer, you still don't completely agree, then wait. Don't move on something when you are not in agreement, unless it is imperative that a decision be made right then. If it must be made, you had better be sure you have heard from heaven, then make the decision and allow God to work on your mate's heart.

As the head of the wife, you are responsible before God for the major decisions, but find a workable means to solve problems before they arise. Your workable solutions may not be the same as Pat's and mine, but for Pat and me, in the financial department, I determine what bills we are going to pay, but I don't carry the checkbook. First of all, I don't want to, and, secondly, I don't like to. So I tell her what bills need to be paid, I lay it all out for her and then I expect her to pay them. She has great skills in money management, and I appreciate that.

She is also highly developed in spending money, and we have had our difficulties over this in the past. Now we come into agreement about how our money is spent.

When it comes to our giving, we have worked out an agreement that has been effective for us. Either of us can give up to an agreed amount to a ministry or to meet a need without talking with the other beforehand. We used to fight over this, but not anymore. It has given us both the freedom we need to obey God and we trust one another in it.

If you go back to the original design, understanding covenant, you realize that it is a one hundred/one hundred situation, not fifty/fifty.

Trust is the basis for every good working relationship between husband and wife, as well as between God and man. Your wife can't really adapt to you if she doesn't trust you. She will always have her guard up. She must also trust God and His Word regarding order in the home. You can't really submit to Christ if you don't trust Him and His Word. Trusting in both cases means you have established in your heart that what has been said is truth and you have chosen to believe it. Truth is the basis for a trusting relationship. Pat and I have learned to trust one another and submit our wills to God and each other. We have learned to speak the truth in love to one another as well as yield to one another's strengths to bring a powerful harmony.

When Battle Lines Are Drawn

A few years ago we faced a personal crisis that had come against our family. There were accusations and lies that needed to be addressed, but it was the kind of situation where I felt I couldn't say the things I wanted to say. It wasn't that I didn't have the guts — I had the guts — but I also had it in my mind that I shouldn't do it.

I remember Pat rising up, strong and bold. She got right into another preacher's face and told him off. God gave me a helpmeet that could stand up and defend me at that moment. There have been other times when I have defended her. So she was simply following my example. This is not a sexist thing; this is about power that comes from truthfulness and unity. The truth was I couldn't do what she did in that instance, but God was still in control. And when she can't do certain things, I can be bold and defend her. The truth is we need each other, but most of all, we need God to be in control!

11
Fatherhood — A Ministry!

Have you ever considered the importance God places on fatherhood? It is one of the central truths to the entire New Testament. For years this significant truth escaped me and, consequently, I failed to take my fatherly role seriously. In fact, in my own troubled state of mind, it seemed easier to leave much of the parental responsibilities to Pat. It seemed like woman's work to me most of the time, anyway.

The major thrust of Jesus' ministry was revealing God as Father to the Jews. While they had revered God, even feared Him, they had difficulty perceiving Him as their heavenly Father. They understood God's sovereignty and knew the law-giving side of Him. But Jesus presented God as their loving, personal Father, One who is all-knowing, all-caring. He declared Him Father God whose chief desire was to bestow His goodness and blessings on His children.

Jesus went about doing good, healing the oppressed, delivering those who were bound, and defying religious traditions. He was moved with compassion to meet people's needs. He said, "If you've seen me, you've seen the Father" (John 14:9, author's paraphrase). Some were outraged by His claims, but He spoke truth. They were witnessing the Father's love in action through Jesus. Can we say the same for ourselves? When our kids see us, can they "see the Father?" Like it or not, our children's fundamental conception of what God is like will be based on their relationship with their father.

Jesus said He was sent first to minister to the Jews, His own people. How often are we running off ministering to everyone else while our own family's needs suffer? Shouldn't our own family be our first ministry? God wanted us to see the essential role fathers play on this earth. Jesus realized His ministry was nothing without the Father and, indeed, His ministry was a revelation of fatherhood in its purest form.

As men of God, we must realize that fatherhood is a vital ministry. Notice I didn't say fathering is ministry. Most men can accomplish that in a few minutes. Fatherhood reaches far beyond what happened one night when the moon was bright and the mood was right! It is more than a few genetic impartations, it is serious ministry.

We live in a confused world where male/female roles are no longer well defined. In fact, they are often perverted. Few of us are prepared for the ministry of fatherhood. Most of our instruction comes inadvertently from untrained, unprepared parents. They do the best they can in their circumstances but, unless they follow godly principles, much of what they teach doesn't work.

Training A Child

The book of Proverbs is one of the best textbooks available on child rearing. It is full of godly wisdom and instruction. Proverbs 22:6 states, **Train up a child in the way he should go: and when he is old, he will not depart from it.** The original root word for *train* "is the term for 'the palate, the roof of the mouth, the gums.'"[1] It is referring to training horses with a bit in their mouth. A bit in a horse's mouth, when used correctly, brings the animal into submission to its master.

This same word also means "developing a thirst."[2] It is referring to a practice that midwives used long ago. In order to prompt a newborn to suck from its mother's breast, the midwife first dipped her finger in date juice, then placed it in the infant's mouth. When she took her finger away, the newborn eagerly suckled its mother's breast. Isn't it interesting that sweetness was used to create the thirst, not harshness.

A third definition for *train* involves "dedication, consecration."[3] So we can see that training involves much more than occasional instruction. It is serious, life-building, character development which involves disciplining our children to follow God's path and do what is right in His eyes. When Jesus told us to make disciples of all men (Matt. 28:19), few of us realized that He was also referring to parenting. A disciple is simply a disciplined student who is taught the ways he should go.

Now let's examine a few more words in Proverbs 22:6. *Child* includes "age of infancy to adolescence,"[4] or all the years the child is under your authority. As long as they are in your home, you are responsible to continue training them.

The word *in* means in keeping with, in cooperation with, and in accordance with. With what? **The way he should go!** In the Hebrew language, *way* "suggests the idea of 'characteristic,' 'manner,' 'mode.'"[5] It is not referring to a specific well-defined road, but rather the road a specific child should travel. In other words, each child has certain characteristics, certain mannerisms, certain traits, and it is up to the parent to train each child individually. Don't make a carbon copy of yourself, his brothers or sisters, or anybody else.

No Robots, Please

If we are going to effectively train our children in the way they should go, we must really know them as individuals first, not as little robots who are programmed to function without feelings or personality.

My two daughters were so different in temperament that I quickly learned to deal with them accordingly. What worked with Candas, a fun-loving child who was always eager to please us, certainly didn't work with strong-willed, independent Cookie. She required a firm hand, often applied to her bottom. All I had to do was look sternly at Candas to get her attention!

Cookie is highly ambitious and self-motivated. We needed to steer her in the right direction, give specific ground rules, and pull the reins tight when she tried to run off course. Candas is different. She tended to be impulsive, flighty and often regretted the consequences of her hasty actions. She was not self-motivated, so we had to remind her continually of truths and exhort her to think things through before doing them. She remembers my warnings "Think, Candy, think! Use your head before you act!" even to this day. Now she sees how it brought stability and common sense to the forefront of her mind, and it still influences her on a daily basis.

Candy's desire to please me worked on her behalf once when she was eighteen and just beginning to explore certain avenues available to her. She and her date were celebrating graduation. They had gone out to a nice restaurant for dinner where wine was offered with their meal. Curious Candy tried the wine, which made her feel so good she later drank vodka. She had never drunk alcohol before, and mixing those two was deadly to her. She got skunk drunk and then extremely sick. Her date dragged her home, up the stairs and put her to bed, unbeknownst to us. The next morning was Sunday and miserable Candy, full of guilt and still a little hazy, knew it was best to be honest and up front with her dad. She knew hiding anything could bring worse results than honestly confessing her misconduct.

So she came downstairs and said, "Daddy, I'm so sorry — I got drunk last night and was sick everywhere." I could see how bad she felt, remembering my own experiences at that age. So I said, "Well, Candy, honey, I'm sorry you've experienced that, but at least I know you'll never want to do it again!" What I didn't realize was that Candas had liked the tipsy feeling she had experienced before getting drunk. In spite of her guilt, she had decided next time she simply wouldn't mix her drinks or drink so much. However, because she respected my opinion, she accepted what I said as fact, and never drank alcoholic beverages again!

Believing in Candas caused her to believe the best about herself. If I had been extremely harsh with her at that moment, and reviled her concerning the evils of drinking, who knows what the outcome would have been. Her personality could have leaned toward alcoholism. The Devil could have easily led her down that path had I not responded the right way to her that morning.

Both Cookie and Candas have become beautiful women who love and serve God faithfully, but they traveled different "ways" to get there. They are the best of friends, yet so different in personality and style. Isn't God grand to create us individually, know us intimately, and guide us personally in the "way" each of us should go? The end result will always be maturity.

While there are basic principles to consider for every child's development, if we train them all the same, without consideration of their unique personalities, and expect them to respond alike, we are in for some serious trouble. The results will be rebellion, resentment and retaliation. And everyone, child and adult alike, will be extremely frustrated in the process.

In a nutshell, training your child in the way they should go means bringing them into submission, as a skilled trainer would handle a fine race horse. Noting that horse's unique strengths and abilities, he develops them for maximum performance. We are to create a thirst in each child for good things, godly things. Recognizing their specific personality, we determine specific techniques that will motivate and mature them. That way they will remain disciplined, always thirsting for good. That way they will remain dedicated to what they have been taught from childhood, and **when he grows old, he will not depart from it.**

12
Big Blessings in Small Packages

It is unfortunate that we live in a world where unborn children are regarded as disposable tissue, a world where media reports of child molestation and abuse are common and child pornography is a highly profitable business. Sadly, it is an obvious fact that a large percentage of adults have neither understanding nor respect for the sanctity and the value of children.

The Bible speaks of children as being from God, and yet, some parents respond to the news of pregnancy as if it were a sentence to eighteen years of hard labor. No one who has ever raised a child would deny that work is involved, but God intended it to be a labor of love! Knowing the Father God, you have to know that if He intended it to be a labor of love, then He also has a plan and a method to accomplish that goal.

Psalm 127:1 says, **Except the Lord build the house, they labor in vain that build it: except the Lord keep the city, the watchman waketh but in vain.** Notice the comparison God establishes between the home and a city. Both can be built in vain. Cities in Bible times always had high walls of protection around them, usually two walls, each several feet thick. Watchmen took turns guarding the city while standing on the walls, thereby protecting the inhabitants from enemy attacks. But God is saying here that no matter how strong it is built, or how well protected it appears to be, it is all in vain without His construction and His protection.

A Father's Fortress

There is also a correlation here between a father's role and the city walls. Those walls performed four functions for the city that we as fathers are to perform for our children. First, they protected the city in the event of an attack. Your children need to feel secure in the knowledge that you are their defender; an enemy has to get through you first; and there is no quit in you when it comes to fighting for them and their rights.

Second, those walls provided a platform from which to be constantly vigilant. Dad, you are the one your children need to be able to trust that you are constantly looking out for their best interests in everything, not just in what is most convenient for you.

Third, those walls supported houses all along the inside perimeter. Are you the strong, mainstay support for your household? Are you dependable when the storms of life try to wash over your little tribe? If not, then you need to be. This is not just financial support, although that is included, but it is also emotional support. You need to be there, active in the household when they need you.

Fourth, those walls contained the gates of the city which were the seat of authority for the community. Whether you like it or not, your children need to be able to look at you as the final authority in their lives, under God of course, and be able to trust your judgments implicitly. The same principle of submission to the Lord in order to be an effective, godly husband applies to your children as well. Your authority over them needs to be rooted and grounded in love and in the wisdom which comes from having spent time with God on their behalf.

Our homes, our families must be built on the love of God, with the foundations set firmly on the Word of God if they are truly to be fortresses God intended them to be, or it is all done in vain.

It is vain for you to rise up early, to sit up late, to eat the bread of sorrows: for so he giveth his beloved sleep (Ps. 127:2). You may work really hard, even get up early in the morning to do all you know to do, or sit up late worrying and trying to take care of all you have, but it will only produce sorrow for you if God isn't your boss and provider. Sleeplessness is usually the result of being overburdened with cares. While it is our responsibility to provide for our family's needs, God is El Shaddai, the One who sees ahead and provides. The reason we can sleep at night is because we know His provision goes beyond the world's system. God is the master contractor of this building project and His blueprints are infallible, His measurements always accurate!

Your Reward

Verse 3, of this same Psalm says, **Lo, children are an heritage of the Lord: and the fruit of the womb is his reward.** Have you regarded your children as rewards lately? Do you recognize them as heritage from God? Both reward and heritage refer to good things, blessings, even wealth. **Every good gift and every perfect gift is from above, and cometh down from the Father of lights, with whom is no variableness, neither shadow of turning** (James 1:17). *No variableness* means does not change even slightly. Therefore, if God said through the Psalmist that children are rewards (like gifts) from Him, and repeated in James that only He gives good and perfect gifts, then whether you can actually see it in your child or not, it is truth! You might have to see it by faith at this moment, but it is still truth! Higher than any truth you can see.

I fully realize there are times when our kids don't appear to be blessings, when they misbehave, cause trouble in the family, create havoc at school and just plain make it hard for you to appreciate them! But so did you at one time or another! I know I gave my parents fits when I was growing up, causing many heartaches! Thank God they still loved me even when I wasn't too loving!

In fact, even when I was supposedly an adult, I caused my parents and Pat's folks fits! I used to blow smoke in Grandma Hagin's face and was downright rude to Brother Hagin, but he loved me and forgave me anyway. I am sure he didn't consider me a blessing or reward material at the time, but the Word was still truth! I became his heritage because I married his daughter, but he had to see it by faith! Being the spiritual man he was, he did just that and kept right on praying for me, and finally got his reward in me hopefully.

Sometimes, the most important thing we can do for our children is accomplished in the spiritual realm. Praying for them helps you stay in faith, helps you treat them as rewards, helps you discipline them in love, and helps you speak the truth over them! Children are our reward whether we can see it or not. Rewards don't come easily in this life, and usually we have to earn them. But here God gives us rewards for a different purpose. Look at Psalm 127:4, **As arrows are in the hand of a mighty man; so are children of the youth.**

"Be Fruitful And Multiply"

What does a mighty man use arrows for? To combat the enemy! God says here that children are like weapons used to combat the enemy. Think about it! The Devil has no ability to reproduce, except by gaining the ungodly man's children. God gives us children, instructs us to train them to love and serve Him and we multiply and increase in strength against the enemy's tactics.

In addition, children often believe God and His Word easier than adults because they aren't so full of doubt and unbelief or traditional thinking. They use what they have learned effectively and operate in faith in a strong way.

When taught right, children are as much a threat to the enemy as adults are. They are like sharpened arrows ready to stop any attack the enemy attempts.

If your ministry only consisted of properly raising your children then, like the servants entrusted with various sums of money while their master was gone, you would have multiplied that which had been entrusted to you several times over. And if you have, **Well done, thou good and faithful servant!** (Matt. 25:21).

Psalm 127:5 states, **Happy is the man that has his quiver full of them; they shall not be ashamed, but they shall speak with the enemies in the gate.** He doesn't have any reason to be ashamed in front of his enemies when he has the finest honed weapons in his quiver. He is a blessed man because not only has he protected his home, but he has taught his family how to protect themselves against the enemy.

Psalm 128 continues in this same vein.

Blessed is every one that feareth the Lord; that walketh in his ways. For thou shalt eat the labour of thine hands: happy shalt thou be, and it shall be well with thee.

Thy wife shall be as a fruitful vine by the sides of thine house; thy children like olive plants round about thy table. Behold, that thus shall the man be blessed that feareth the Lord.

The Lord shall bless thee out of Zion: and thou shalt see the good of Jerusalem all the days of thy life; Yea, thou shalt see thy children's children, and peace upon Israel.

That is quite a promise! Our wives will be like fruitful vines growing by the sides of the house and our children like olive plants round about our table. If a man didn't understand the importance of olive plants,[1] the powerful truth in that verse would be overlooked. Olives may seem small and insignificant, but they have a wide variety of uses and are considered a valuable commodity to the Middle Eastern countries.

Young olive trees only bear olives after seven years of growth, reaching maturity after about fourteen years. Once the olive tree reaches its maturity, its fruitfulness lasts for many years. In fact, its longevity is one of the remarkable characteristics of the tree. It lives and bears fruit for centuries!

An old olive tree is often seen with several young shoots springing up all around from its roots. No doubt this is the picture the Psalmist had in mind when he wrote that verse.

Today in the Orient, olive oil is used in place of butter most of the time. It is also the main cooking oil used in the majority of homes.Even the wood from an olive tree is often used in the East. Oriental carpenters are fond of using it, especially in the construction of cabinets. King Solomon had the cherubim of the temple, the inner and outer doors and the posts of the sanctuary all made of olive wood.

Olive oil was used almost exclusively for fueling lamps during Bible times. Even today it is used in Bible lands to manufacture soap.

Olive oil was considered to be one of the great sources of wealth in King Solomon's days. It was also used for anointing the body both for healing and for various religious ceremonies.

Historically, the olive tree has been considered a symbol of peace since the time of Noah. When a dove was sent out from the ark, it returned with an olive leaf in its mouth! And throughout the Bible, oil is used to symbolize the Holy Spirit. It was also considered a symbol of abundance — the lack of it a sign of want.

So when God refers to our children as olive plants around our table, He is speaking of great wealth, of goodness, of continual fruitfulness, of productivity, and longevity, of valued products, of great necessity, of peaceful promises, of the anointing of the Holy Spirit, of abundance, and of no lack! Next time you look at your children, consider how God looks at them and thank Him for all He's provided!

Reread the description of God's blessing to the man that fears Him in Psalm 128:4-6. *Fear* means to reverence God,[2] acknowledging Him as the Almighty God, Creator of heaven and earth, the Most High God. It also means to reverence His Word, for Jesus is the Word. Isn't it interesting that reverencing God is included in these psalms about families? The promises of blessings, long life, and grandchildren and peace are all connected with recognizing the truth about your home, your wife and children. The blessings are given to you as a man but, first, you must recognize God in your home, honor Him, and serve Him.

Then you must see your children and wife in the right perspective, as valued gifts in your life. When you see them in this fashion, you will treat them with respect and love. The blessing of God will continue to your children's children and peace will reign supreme!

Yes, it's true — big blessings often come in small packages!

13
Train Up Or Trip Up!

There are many good books on the market about parenting. Often they focus on sound, Biblical principles concerning discipline. This chapter is not intended to cover that area in its entirety, but to illuminate certain principles I used when approaching this matter with my own kids.

As I wrote before, my father's type of discipline was to deal severely with me. I strongly resented his methods of correcting me, so I rebelled even more. Rebellion comes when rules are established without relationship. My dad and I didn't have anything like a decent relationship until just a few years ago. So, I resented his rules, disobeyed them and did my own thing.

The children of Israel were much the same way. According to God's Word, they were stiff-necked, rebellious people. They refused to obey His commandments time after time and refused to enter into and abide in a relationship with God. Therefore, they continually sinned.

Only God's mercy and, on several occasions, Moses' intercession kept them alive. Yet they still wandered in the wilderness for 40 years because of their rebellion and sin.

The Root Of The Problem

A careful look at the reason behind their rebellion reveals the root of the problem. They refused to have a *personal relationship* with God Almighty. They wanted Moses to speak to God face to face for them, and get their instructions from Him. No wonder God said He would create a people who had His laws in their hearts. He wants us to love Him and serve Him out of hearts full of love and thanksgiving. And because He has blessed us so much, our hearts respond to Him and our desire is to refrain from sin.

Jesus said, **I always do that which pleases the Father** (John 8:29). Where did this determination come from? From the Father Himself! It was a loving Father-Son relationship in action, revealed to the entire world.

Our children should be seeking the same thing Jesus did — a single-minded desire to please their father. To accomplish that in our children's lives, as fathers, we are responsible for initiating the relationship with our kids, not vice versa. They will respond to discipline when love, affection and relationship have been established beforehand. It was essential for Jesus to fulfill the Father's commands; it is just as essential for our children.

I remember when I was growing up my dad had an old boat that needed restoration. Guess who was elected to restore the thing? Me! This old boat had layers of paint, pitch and barnacles. Everyday after school I had to work on that old boat, scraping layers of paint and barnacles off that thing. I hated it! I was churning on the inside. If Dad had just done it with me, it would have been a great time of fun and fellowship together while we worked.

But one thing Dad did do during the boat scraping job changed my whole way of thinking about work. I will be eternally grateful for what he taught me! He taught me how to have fun working!

I scoffed at the idea at first. How could scraping by the hour on that boat all by myself be any fun? Dad got his stopwatch out and gave it to me. Then he said, "Start scraping and see how much you can scrape in five minutes." I did a little bitty section in the allotted time. Then he said,

"Now see if you can do more in the next five minutes." I responded to the challenge and worked harder. Pretty soon I was doubling and tripling my productivity on that old boat. It became fun to see how I could compete with my former record and before long that old boat was clear and clean, and ready for refinishing.

Amateur Or Professional?

What Dad taught me was a principle which works in anything you do. Amateurs compete with each other, but professionals compete with themselves. Whatever it is I undertake, I am always seeing if I can do a better, faster and more effective job than before. This is real self-improvement! It is healthy and productive and keeps your heart right at the same time. And you never stop growing.

I owe my dad a great deal for teaching me that principle. Yes, it could have been better had he worked alongside me, and perhaps our relationship would have improved then, instead of later. But what good does it do to live in the past? Dad did the best he could at the time, and he taught me many valuable lessons that still influence my life today. For that I am very grateful!

One important factor to consider in training up our children is that the punishment ought to fit the wrong actions. It should be appropriate for the child's age and personality as well as teach them about the Biblical principles they violated by misbehaving. Some kids simply despise talks and would rather have a quick spanking to get the whole thing over in a hurry. If the child doesn't learn why his actions were wrong, then he only learned the immediate consequences of sin, not the long term penalties. And if the punishment doesn't fit the crime, he will resent you for it even when he knows he deserves it. Many times I received beatings but never understood why what I did was so wrong. God's Word always shows us the entire picture of sin's consequences as examples, so we won't make the same mistakes. We need to teach our children accordingly.

For instance, in innocence, a boy might look at a pornographic magazine, but soon his inflamed curiosity will lead to more. And if he continues in that, he will begin experimenting with the same things he first looked at so innocently. Soon he will be hooked on porno, and the thrill of the moment will lead him to more and more. Sexual sins will abound in his life and affect or possibly ruin his future.

Likewise, a young girl might start reading the graphic romance novels of today, and soon her natural desire for an intimate relationship is fanned into an obsession of expectations and desires and unhealthy motivations which could ruin her life just as surely as pornography can. In fact, we can justifiably label these books *emotional* pornography. Just because they are more acceptable socially, don't be deceived. They are just as damaging to the soul as their visual cousin.

Spanking the kid because he looked at the pornography or read the romance book out of curiosity isn't going to help. All it will do is affect their little behinds momentarily. Instruction is needed or their curiosity may be increased. They will look and explore again, wondering why you were so upset at those things.

Instruction Plus Discipline = Training

Instruction *must* accompany any form of discipline or punishment inflicted on a child, but it should be in line with, and in light of, the Word of God. Read it to them, or allow them to read it out loud in your presence. Let them ask questions, and be sure they understand the long-term consequences of sin, not only that it is wrong. With pornography of either kind, for example, they must realize it will always bring harm. It isn't something they are simply too young to see.

In Proverbs 31, Solomon recounts the prophesy his mother Bathsheba taught him concerning women and sexual things. When he says, "my son," he is talking to the person who is building the family name. The king was saying more here than meets the eye. He was saying, "Son, you are the builder of the family name. Keep it built right when it comes to relationship. Watch where you spend your strength (referring to sexual strength). Beware of the pitfalls of drinking, how it affects your judgment." He continues by describing a virtuous woman and the importance she has in a man's life.

King Solomon was using the opportunity to instruct his son on much more than sexual matters. He wisely used the opportunity to instruct him on life-changing issues. You see, instruction cannot be accomplished by a spanking alone!

However, if instruction were the only way to make disciples of our children, the only way to train them up in the way they should go, the many verses regarding spanking would not be in the Bible at all.

Proverbs 29:15, **The rod and reproof give wisdom: but a child left to himself bringeth his mother to shame.** Notice we are to use the both the rod *and* reproof. We cannot discipline a child effectively when we only use one method, either what the Bible calls the rod, or spanking, or just reproof. It takes both.

The words *a child left* mean, left to their sin nature.[1] Shame comes to the child's mother when a child is left to live by their own set of rules. Children are not born with an implanted set of rules. They will either develop their own, or you can teach them yours. A child may shame their mother but, as the father, you will be held accountable, too.

The Rod Plus Reproof = Wisdom

How then does the rod and reproof, or correction, bring wisdom? First of all, *when* it is done is key. Proverbs 13:24 says, **He that spareth the rod hateth his son; but he that loveth him chasteneth him betimes.** *Betimes* means "early."[2] We could take that to mean early in your child's development, use the rod or you aren't really loving him correctly. Now, nobody likes to spank a little toddler who is still running around in diapers, but that is the time to start! Early, before disobedience becomes rebellion, and gets out of hand.

Physical correction should be done not only early, but prayerfully. That is, not when you are too angry to pray, but after you have prayed and the anger has subsided. Just send the child to his room to wait until you have fully prepared yourself. Love must be established before and after a rod is used to discipline the child.

A rod simply means a switch or stick, not a two by four! My dad used a big old belt he had. Boy, those belts can sting! But since the Word specifically refers to the rod, that is the right way to go.

Proverbs 22:15 says, **Foolishness is bound in the heart of a child; but the rod of correction shall drive it far from him.** Notice it is a rod of correction, not a rod of beating. The purpose isn't to literally beat the kid till he has welts on his rear, but to use a stick to make a sufficiently strong impression so as to correct their wrong behavior.

There is a modern line of thinking that says any time you hit a child it is abuse. That is simply not true. Many of the people proposing that philosophy have never themselves had any children, or are reacting to their own emotions. The Word of God is very clear. Physical correction is a vital part of discipline for a child, and the parent who refuses to administer it actually loves their child less than the parent who will.

Let's face it, kids can be foolish at times. They do foolish things because they are kids, not adults. But even adults do foolish things from time to time. Sometimes we see kids doing what we do and react to them, when it is ourselves that need the correction first! Sometimes the habits they have learned become such reminders of our own shortcomings, we are irritated with them. If you don't correct your own actions, they will hear your instruction and feel that rod on their behinds, yet sooner or later they will come to resent you and will imitate you anyway! Remember, you are instructing them day and night, whether you are aware of it or not.

A Spiritual Battle

I said earlier we need to discipline prayerfully not out of our anger. But what about a wrong attitude or what if your child is actually acting badly because of spiritual forces influencing him? If you haven't prayed, how will you know whether to take authority over a harassing spirit, or spank his little behind? You can't spank out a demon!

I am not saying your child may be possessed, but he could be oppressed or harassed by demonic influences! Spanking and reproof won't get the job done. You must use the Name of Jesus like you mean it, in faith, understanding your rightful authority as that child's parent. If the child is spiritually mature enough to take some actions themselves, you will know that through prayer, too.

If you haven't trained your children spiritually, you must realize it is just as important as any spanking or instruction you will ever give them. I trained our children through family devotions early every morning because I wanted to get the Word into them. We would speak the Word in our house and pray together, and as a result, they brought other kids from the neighborhood over for our devotion times. The neighbor kids got saved, filled with the

Spirit, healed, etc. The neighbors were drawn to our family because of the love. That is what family is all about.

Sure, I was tough on my kids, especially early on, before I was following after God. I found the more spiritually developed I became, the less I wanted to spank my kids, but I still had to take action when they acted up. It was just as hard on me as it was on them — hurt me as much as them — but it still needed to be done.

Even though I was a strict disciplinarian, our family remained close knit. They may not have liked the rod when it was skillfully applied to their behinds, but they appreciate it now when they are adults and have their own children.

As children, even though I spanked them and corrected them often, they still thought their Daddy could do anything. I remember one time when Brother Hagin was teasing Cookie because she was talking about all I could do. He said, "Cookie, you just think your daddy's something, don't ya?" She said, "Yep." He said, "I bet you think he hung the moon." She said, "Yeah, he did, and we went up there and had a picnic, too!" And she began to tell him off because he laughed and scoffed at her!

You might think she was just making all that up, but in her mind, the fellowship we had as a family brought her great delight, even to the furthest points of the moon! So all the spankings in the world didn't stop that family love and fellowship from flowing.

Our kids weren't rebellious because we had love and fellowship, in addition to rules and regulations. We spent time together to such an extent that there was hardly a private place in our house we could go! And many times our kids, when they were young, all piled on our bed and romped together with us.

Aids, Adds, Assures

I really think loving discipline aids rather than hinders family relationships. It also adds a dimension of caring and responsibility that is obvious to our children. This, in turn, gives them an assurance of our love and commitment to them. Our relationship with God is sometimes one of Father/child and sometimes Abba-Daddy, a lovely-dovey sort of thing. As Father, He may be stern, warning us, correcting us, or simply instructing us. As Daddy, He may hold us and kiss our cheeks. It depends on the need.

So it should be with our children! Just as we can come boldly into the throne room of our Father, so our children need to know they can come boldly into our presence for their needs to be met. And when they just want to play or fellowship with us, we need to be available for that, too, just as God is always available for us, to love and fellowship with us, and have fun with us.

If God didn't discipline us, we would wonder if He loved us, since the Word shows us clearly He chastens those He loves. (Heb. 12:6.) When your children act up, if you don't discipline them, sooner or later, they will wonder if you really love them. (Have you ever noticed that some days it seems they are just begging for that spanking?) Some day they may ask you why you didn't correct those bad habits in them, why you didn't care enough to develop the right character in them, why you didn't help them when they were hurting so desperately and needed your attention. I wouldn't want to be the man who hears those things.

If we don't train our children up right, somebody will some day. It may be the world's system or the prison system, but somebody will govern those who refuse to govern themselves. And the only way someone learns to govern himself is through his parents or the adults responsible for his training.

Train up or you trip up in the end! And so will your child! I am so glad my heavenly Father loves me enough to correct me when I am wrong. He has shown us the example — now it is up to us to carry it out!

14
Pay Attention, Son!

When I was young man, I was so hardheaded in so many areas my dad often had to deal with me severely. I was as stubborn as an old mule. I reminded myself of the Scripture:

> **I will instruct thee and teach thee in the way which thou shalt go: I will guide thee with mine eye. Be ye not as the horse or as the mule, which has no understanding: whose mouth must be held in with bit and bridle, lest they come near unto thee.**
>
> **Psalm 32:8-9**

God says He wants to instruct us so we will do right, but, for our part, we need to be easily entreated, not hardheaded and stubborn.

Years ago a joke went around about a man trying to get an old mule to cooperate with him. He shouted until he was hoarse with no result. Finally, in desperation he took the mule to a mule trainer known to have success with even the most stubborn of animals. After shelling out good hard cash, he turned his mule over to the trainer who tied the mule to a corral post. Then the trainer picked up a two-by-four, walked over to the mule and promptly whacked him right between the eyes. The mule's knees buckled and tears seemed to well up in his eyes. The mule's owner was furious. "What do you think you're doing?" he protested. "Just watch," replied the trainer whereupon he whispered in the mule's ear. The mule kinda nodded his head and went trotting over to where he had been told to go.

The owner was astonished, "That's amazing! All you did was whisper in his ear and he obeyed you. But if that's all it took, why in the world did you hit him with that two-by-four?" "Well," replied the trainer, "First, you gotta get his attention!"

Sometimes we face the same challenge with our children. It is not that they are unwilling, it is just that we don't have their attention. Of course I am not recommending we beat them over the head, but there are ways of training them which capture their attention and obtain the desired results.

Military drill sergeants demand certain performances from their units because they know it could make the difference between life and death. They drill their men daily, hour by hour, teaching them how to handle weapons skillfully and how to respond automatically in certain situations. The soldier is expected to conform whether he wants to or not. That drill sergeant knows he must get each soldier to respond instantly and without hesitation when he gives a command. His purpose may seem distorted to the soldier in training, but the training is for his own good, because his life depends upon it.

If a soldier is allowed to remain stubborn and unresponsive, he could be killed. A drill sergeant doesn't say, "I'd appreciate it if when I holler 'hit the dirt' and you can find it in your heart to agree, you would be so kind as to do it." No, he trains and drills them so much it becomes automatic. They hear "hit the dirt," and they are on the ground, pronto, without even thinking!

While I am not suggesting we act like drill sergeants with our kids, they must recognize the instruction we give them is for their own good and could make the difference between life and death. Our kids need to understand that some training is going to be hard on the flesh, but it brings vast rewards in the future. They need to recognize there is a real enemy out there who desires their very life, namely Satan. Responding instantly to your commands will train them to respond quickly to God's voice. When you teach them God's Word, they will begin to recognize the enemy's deception. They will understand God's ways, and forsake evil.

A Fundamental Principle

There is an important principle here I don't want to overlook or slight. We need to understand that in order to recognize evil, to discern the work of the enemy, we must be steeped in God's Word, studying good not evil, the ways of the Lord not the Devil. Here is the principle: *You can recognize the counterfeit by knowing intimately the real.*

Those who are experts in recognizing counterfeit money don't study all the various types of counterfeit cash, but rather they spend hours getting intimately knowledgeable of the real thing. That way, when counterfeit cash comes their way, it is easy to spot because it is different from what they are so familiar with.

Before Israel took possession of the Promised Land, God gave them certain commands designed to establish this principle in their hearts.

> Now these are the commandments, the statutes and the judgments, which the Lord your God commanded to teach you, that ye might do them in the land whither ye go to possess it:
> That thou mightest fear the Lord thy God, to keep all his statutes and his commandments, which I command thee, thou, and thy son, and thy son's son, all the days of thy life; and that thy days may be prolonged.
> Hear, therefore, O Israel, and observe to do it; that it may be well with thee, and that ye may increase mightily, as the Lord God of thy fathers hath promised thee, in the land that floweth with milk and honey.

Hear, O Israel: The Lord our God is one Lord: And thou shalt love the Lord thy God with all thine heart: and with all thy soul, and with all thy might.

And these words, which I command thee this day, shall be in thine heart; And thou shalt teach them diligently unto thy children, and shalt talk of them when thou sittest in thine house, and when thou walkest by the way, and when thou liest down, and when thou risest up.

Deuteronomy 6:1-7

Notice the use of the word *all* in verse five. God expects us to sell out to Him, give Him our all! Next, He says His Words shall be in our hearts, down on the inside of us where they are protected and producing results as we draw upon them for instruction. Then we are to teach them diligently to our children, while we sit in our own living rooms. Next He says we are to talk of God's Word when we walk with our children, and at their bedtime, and at the breakfast table.

God commanded us as fathers to teach our children His Word all day long, whether we are at home, at play, or on the way! Teaching should occur in every facet of their lives, whether it be by our words or by our actions. Have you ever realized everything we do teaches our kids something? They are going to observe our ways regardless of whether we want them to notice or not. We must learn to set the right example, because they are bound to follow in our footsteps someday and do what we have taught them.

Deuteronomy 6:20 says, ...**when thy son asketh thee in the time to come....** This assumes you and your kids are on speaking terms. If you aren't communicating, how can you effectively teach them? Our words are vital and our actions must illustrate what we are saying.

When thy son asketh thee means he feels free to ask questions and he has seen or heard something that has

154

created a question in his mind. Children are naturally curious and, sometimes, those continual questions can be irritating, but we should be thanking God for the opportunity to share His truths with them. **And when thy son asketh thee,...saying, What mean the testimonies... which the Lord our God hath commanded you?** (v. 20).

...and the statutes, and the judgments.... In other words, the son wants to know more about God, more about His Words, His Ways. Kids need understanding about laws, whether they are God's laws, your household rules or man's laws. They need to know the difference, the reasoning behind them, and the consequences of not obeying them.

...which the Lord our God hath commanded you? Then thou shalt say unto thy son, We were Pharaoh's bondmen in Egypt; and the Lord brought us out of Egypt with a mighty hand....
Deuteronomy 6:21

Were we not all brought out of bondage, delivered from the power of sin and death?

And the Lord shewed signs and wonders, great and sore, upon Egypt, upon Pharaoh and upon all his household, before our eyes:...(v. 22). Can't you too testify of the miracles you have seen right before your eyes? **And he brought us out from thence that he might bring us in, to give us the land which he sware unto our fathers** (v. 23). Tell them how God's redemption works, how He always delivers us from something, unto something far better. Tell them of His promises, how they are always yes and amen in Christ, how serving God rather than Satan brings benefits far beyond what the world has to offer.

And the Lord commanded us to do all these statutes, to fear the Lord our God, for our good always, that he might preserve us alive, as it is at this day.
Deuteronomy 6:24

Are you alive to God? Then you can tell them that He has given you eternal life, abundant life in Jesus; that once death worked in you, but now God's life flows through you, preserving you. These are the things we are to declare to our children, when we are in our homes, when they are lying down, when they are getting up, when they are going someplace, all the time.

A Grandfather's Example

In my own life, it was my grandfather who taught me about God when I was a young child. My dad went overseas to the war during the first five years of my life, so Mom and I lived with my grandparents.

My grandfather was an old Spirit-filled Methodist preacher who joined the Pentecostal folks. Every day he read the Bible to me, taught me from the Word. Every day he told me stories, every day we prayed. He told me Bible stories about Abraham, Isaac, Jacob, David, Samuel and Solomon. Those stories were great, but he also told me stories of what God had done for him. I didn't realize it then, but he planted seeds of faith in me that would last forever.

Grandfather presented God to me in a very real fashion, where He was not someone far away, but a very real person who worked in our lives. I saw how He worked with David, with Samson, with the Bible heroes, but then I saw how He worked in Grandfather's life.

He told me of the time some folks were coming to kill him — they didn't like what he preached and had even tarred and feathered him once. This time, an old scrawny rooster stuck his head up on the porch, and began to crow. My grandfather understood everything that old rooster was saying. God warned him through the rooster saying, "Leave, I've made a way of escape for you."

Grandfather picked up his Bible off the altar, walked out the side door and there was a man with a buckboard and a team of horses. He jumped on the buckboard, and the driver took him down to the train station where another man with a ticket was ready for him. Through his stories I saw the delivering power of God so clearly, so precisely. He showed me how God always causes us to triumph. (2 Cor. 2:14.)

Grandfather also showed me God was his supplier. He told me of the time he had been out preaching and had to use all the offering he had received just to get back home to his wife and four kids. There was no food in the house, no money to buy anything. But he had made an agreement with God: "I'll go where you want me to go, but it's up to You to supply my needs and those of my family." He used to sing this little song, "Jesus said, 'If you'll go, I'll go with you, preach the Gospel, and I'll preach it with you.'" That was how he lived, preaching the Gospel, with God supplying the needs of him and his family.

This time when he had come home, there was no food, no money in the house, and he had no money left from the trip. He had been out, obeyed God, preached the Gospel, done all he knew to do. My grandmother said, "What will we do?" He said, "We're gonna act like God's Word is so. He's my supplier. Call the kids in the house." She called them in and said, "What will we do now?" He said, "Set the table." Next she asked, "Now what do we do?" He said, "Let's sit down — we're going to offer thanks."

So they sat down at the table; he lifted up his head and hands and began to praise God. Reminding Him of his promise, He said, "Lord, You said if I'd go, You'd go with me; if I'd preach the Gospel, You'd preach it with me. You said You'd supply my every need, and I want to thank You, Father, that You always honor Your Word."

After he prayed that prayer, he opened his eyes to a full course meal sitting on the table. It had never happened before, and it never happened again, but a woman preparing a meal across the street was just finishing up when the Spirit of God spoke up on the inside of her and said, "I have need of that, take it over to that preacher's house." She walked in with that meal and put it on the table while Grandfather was giving thanks!

I saw the delivering power through my grandfather's life. It pierced my heart so that even later, when I had gone astray, I couldn't get away from the truth. Those stories and the Bible stories forever lived in me, stirring my heart. God's Word never returns to Him void!

Years later, when I was eleven years old and paralyzed with polio, I remembered Grandfather's stories about God's delivering power. I was so stricken, laying there, scared silly in that hospital bed watching the boy next to me who was in an iron lung. I cried out, "God of my grandfather...." I knew he knew Him, so I said, "God of my grandfather, I need Your help now — I need it now!" And while I was crying out to God there, my grandfather was at home, praying in the Spirit. Something hit me in the head and went all the way through my feet, and a week later I walked out totally healed by the power of God!

I firmly believe I am what I am today because of the influence of my grandfather's word on my early life. He even told me how he had prayed for me when I was in my mother's womb. What a powerful effect our words have on other's lives, and especially children, during those first highly impressionable years of their lives.

How vital and important it is that we share ourselves and not just our philosophies with our children!

Because Grandfather told me how he had faced dire circumstances in his life and how God had delivered him from crisis and calamity, I developed faith in God's delivering power that has always stuck with me. I know I need never be embarrassed or ashamed of the God I serve, regardless of how others try to ridicule or belittle. I know He works on my behalf, just as He did my grandfather's, just as He did with Abraham, Isaac and Jacob. Grandfather's faith was passed on to me because he taught me just as the Word says for fathers and grandfathers to do. I thank God for his obedience!

After my Dad returned from the war I walked away from the things of God for awhile, but God's truths never left me. They were always pulling me back to the principles I had been taught as a young lad! But I returned! How true the proverb is: **And when he is old he will not depart from it.** (22:6)

Fathers, grandfathers, present God to your children. Declare His truths to them even while they are in the womb; speak them as the youngsters lie in their crib, as they begin to crawl. When they take those first few steps, teach them that God orders their steps, and when they are able to run, let them see we are running a good race with Jesus. Use every opportunity you have to speak of God's goodness and love to your children, and let that love work in you. When your child has blown it, allow him to see forgiveness and acceptance as well as punitive action.

It has been said that children usually identify God with their fathers. If you have been harsh and severe in your treatment, the child often sees God that way. If you have been wimpy and ineffective, God will be perceived the same. How do your children see God in your actions? Can they identify with Him lovingly or do they hide from Him in fear? It is up to you to present the right image, just as Jesus did for us!

15
Grandchildren Are Grand!

Before my first grandson J.D. was born, I had no idea what joy grandparenting could bring to my life. At one time I felt a little apprehensive about it, thinking that being a grandfather might make me seem or feel older. I didn't want to be viewed as an "old grandpa." Pat however, faced the reality of grandparenthood with anticipation and joy from the minute she heard Cookie was pregnant, but it took me a while to adjust to that new aspect of life.

Now that I have four wonderful grandchildren, I realize my concerns were groundless. My grandchildren bring great joy and delight to my heart whenever I am around them or even think of them. And I have found that, as a grandparent, I have great influence on that younger generation. In fact, I really believe grandparents can deposit spiritual impartations and truths in a greater dimension and with a different emphasis than parents can.

Proverbs 13:22 states, **A good man leaveth an inheritance to his children's children....** While I realize this pertains specifically to financial inheritance, much in the soulish realm can be left to them as well.

I think the emotional security my grandfather gave me through his unconditional love and acceptance meant just as much to me as the spiritual truths he imparted to me. He made an unforgettable deposit inside me nothing or no one can ever take away. One can lose financial inheritances or misspend them, but spiritual inheritances and soulish impartations last forever. And they are often passed on to the next generation. (It doesn't have to just be the sins and iniquities that are passed on!)

As a grandfather, I probably have more spiritual influence on my grandchildren than their own parents do. Children have a tendency to resent their parents' attempts to develop certain traits in their lives. Grandparents can appeal to them from a logical and emotional level as well as a spiritual. We don't have the same responsibility to see their little characters develop, nor do we have to see them follow through on chores, etc. While Pat and I do discipline the grandkids when they are in our care, it is still not the same as parenting.

A part of what grandparents bring to their grandkids are living stories — something their parents can't deliver as effectively. My granddaddy left me a wealth of living stories that still minister to me today!

Another thing grandparents can do is help their grandchildren see things from another viewpoint. I often wonder where I would be today if my grandfather hadn't talked me out of killing my Dad when I was in my teens. My anger and resentment was so overwhelming I was actually convinced I had a foolproof plan to take my dad's life without anyone knowing who had done it. Somehow my grandfather sensed I was about to make a severe mistake. He logically approached me, got the truth out of me, and talked some sense into me. If he hadn't, I would be a much different man today, and I would be telling the story from a prison cell. The Devil is a liar, but I didn't know it was his influence that induced me to plan a murder. I would have brought disaster, shame and sorrow to my family if Grandpa hadn't prayed and intervened. I would never have answered God's call to the ministry, nor fulfilled His plan for my life.

Living Stories

Grandfather also showed me the importance of marrying the woman God wants you to marry! How I appreciate his wisdom in demonstrating before my eyes what marriage was all about. He probably had one of the greatest marriages I have ever witnessed! My grandmother was a faithful, virtuous woman who loved God and Grandfather with all her might.

Grandfather loved to tell me how he and Grandma met. He was a Methodist minister who got filled with the Spirit and wanted to go to Bible school. Back in those days, they only ran Bible schools for a few weeks at a time because most people couldn't afford much time away from their other responsibilities.

He went to Hot Springs, Arkansas, to a Bible school. One day, as he was getting ready to attend classes, he was shaving and the Lord spoke to him. (Isn't it strange how God gets us in position to hear him?) There he was, with shaving cream all over his face, when the Lord spoke to him and said, "I want you to go back to Louisiana where you held that meeting and marry that little Caber girl you met there." He had met her, but had never gone out with her. She was of French descent.

Grandfather said, "Now, Lord, I'm not sure I want to do that. It's bad enough being beat up and run out of town for preaching, even had my tent burned down on me. I'm just not sure having a wife with me will work. What if they beat her, too? I don't think I could restrain myself if someone harmed my wife. It's rough enough being out there by myself like that." He finished shaving, carrying on this conversation, and when he started out the door, the Lord again said, "I want you to go back down there and marry her."

Grandfather knew he had to settle this issue, so he turned around and started back into the house. He had his Bible in his hand, so he said, "Lord, I'm gonna throw this Bible on the bed." (The pages are still bent today where it fell open that day.) He hauled off and threw that Bible over his shoulder, across the room, onto the bed. It went tumbling, pages going over and over, until it came open to the passage about Jesus at the marriage feast! Grandfather knew he had better obey God! (Don't use this as a regular method of hearing from God, however!)

The next week he headed out for Louisiana. God also spoke to my Grandmother at the same time, saying, "George Harrison is coming to marry you." He even told her what day he was coming, and what train he would be on. She was there to meet him and they married soon after that!

Over the years, I watched my grandparents together. Every day they began their day sitting down together. She would read from the Bible, then they would pray together. He would read throughout the day, quoting Scriptures all the time, but they always started their day together in the Word and prayer. They were married nearly 70 years before they went to be with the Lord. Seventy years together, reading and praying, living out God's will for their lives.

They were as loving in their later years as in their former. Grandmother faithfully kept house for him, cooked great meals, laid out his clothes, waited on him hand and foot. I don't know how he got her to do so much for him! I have tried — and even schemed — to get Pat just to scratch my back for years. I even tried to tell her she had that ministry, but she didn't buy it!

My grandparents continually shouted the victory every day of their long lives. What a legacy they left me through their love, their example of marriage, of a godly home! They devoted their lives to God and each other. To them family was vital. They instilled a vision for the family that my parents couldn't give me. No, not because there wasn't love in our home — there was — but Dad didn't serve the Lord until late in his life, so there was a difference.

My grandparents gave me security when Dad was overseas during the war. They gave me hope for the future, faith for today, love forever. Don't underestimate what you have to give to your own grandchildren! They might be more open to your wisdom than you think! I know for years my grandfather probably didn't see any tangible evidence of his spiritual and emotional impartations in my life. Oh, maybe now and then, he saw some little spark of truth and light come forth but, for the most part, it wasn't until I went to Bible school myself that they saw a change in me.

So leave a living legacy to your grandchildren. Bring life into their lives and hearts through your experiences with the Lord. Teach them God's ways through your ways, and love them with all of your heart. Oh, they're grand, all right, *grand*children who accept you as you are and love you for it! — *grand*children who listen to you with baited breath, who don't mind your repetitious stories and who laugh at your dumb jokes. They are grand, and they have a way of making you feel grand yourself!

16
In Closing...

We live in an hour when godly men, husbands, and fathers *must* take a stand for truth and righteousness. While I haven't always lived my life the way God intended, I have come to realize God's mercy is fresh and new each morning. His grace is sufficient for all He has called me to do as a man, as a husband, as a father and grandfather.

When God entered into covenant with Abraham, He entrusted enormous blessings to that man and his seed. We are of the seed of Abraham because we are in Jesus, and those same blessings are available to us. Spiritual riches and material riches were imparted unto Abraham because God knew He had found a man with four characteristics vital to His plan of redemption of mankind. First, God could trust Abraham who was faithful to his word. Second, Abraham would follow His plan — he was obedient. Third, He saw in Abraham a man who would highly esteem his wife. Fourth, Abraham would teach His children godly principles as well. If you are looking for a blueprint or formula for doing the job of being God's man for yourself, your wife and your family, you couldn't find a much better strategy than Abraham's four point plan.

Abraham was fruitful in every aspect of his life once he operated within the covenant God had created for him. He was faithful to God, even when God asked him to offer up his beloved son Isaac. He was tried and true, a man who stood for what was right when others wouldn't.

As the seed of Abraham, we have been left an inheritance that is unshakable, impenetrable, incorruptible and unending. Now it is our turn to pass that heritage on to our children, and our children's children, until we meet the Lord or He returns for His Bride.

I have attempted to impart some truths in this book regarding your role as man and husband, as father and grandfather. My desire is for us to bring glory and honor unto God as men of God were intended to do. We see so little in the world today to look up to, to honor, or even to admire. Men have become objects of ridicule in television sitcoms, Hollywood movies, silly cartoons and senseless comic strips. Few examples of real men who stand up for godly truths are ever reported in newspapers or illustrated on TV!

Instead, what we have seen are weaklings who are henpecked and ridiculed, or muscular macho men who advertise beer and condone "safe sex." When are men going to take a stand? When are we going to see men who aren't afraid to be tough yet tender when needed? When are we going to see men who openly profess love for God, for their wives and family, and for their country?

When are we as men going to say no to sick satires on manliness, say no to pornography, say no to perverted jokes and filthy movies? When are we going to restore respect for womanhood, for motherhood, for family values and godliness? When are we going to reflect God's image of manhood, to stand up and be counted for what is right and good?

We are a chosen generation, called by God to be men of God, to be husbands who live like Christ did, and fathers who bring our Heavenly Father's love into our homes and churches! Yes, we will stand out in a crowd when we decide to live according to God's standards, not because we are weird or overzealous, but because we represent truth and honesty — because we speak with boldness and grace — because we are living epistles of God's living Word operating through us — because we choose to walk humbly before our God, yet with heads held high, knowing our rights as men of God, as kings and priests.

Yes, men, it is time to take our stand, to join the plan, and to be the man that God has planned! It's time to be <u>real</u> men, husbands, and fathers! You can do it — with His help!

Endnotes

Chapter 3
[1]Wilson, p. 98.
[2]Wilson, p. 114.

Chapter 4
[1]Strong, "Greek," entry #5343, p. 75.

Chapter 5
[1]Strong, "Hebrew," entry #3335, p. 51.
[2]"n.m. pl. abstr. emph. life." Noun, masculine; *plural abstract emphasis.* Brown, p. 313.
[3]The preceding information in the section "A Physical Basis" is based on the following: Statements by Donald M. Joy, Ph.D., Professor in Human Development and Christian Education, Asbury Theological Seminary, Asbury Michigan, in a Focus on the Family radio interview with Dr. James Dobson, n.d.; *Bonding Relationships in the Image of God* by Dr. Donald M. Joy (Waco: Word Books, 1985), pp. 89, 90; and "Debate: Does `Wiring' Rule Emotion, Skill?" by Karen S. Peterson in USA TODAY, Jul. 8, 1992, p. 1A.
[4]Strong, "Hebrew," entry #5970.
[5]Strong, "Hebrew," entry #1523.

Chapter 6
[1]Vine, s.v. "strongholds," Vol. 4, p. 85.
[2]*Webster's New World Dictionary,* 3d College Ed., s.v. "fortress."
[3]Vine, s.v. "grace," Vol. 2, pp. 169, 170.
[4]Strong, "Greek," based on entry #2852.

Chapter 7
[1]Strong, "Hebrew," based on "help" and "meet," Gen. 2:18, entry #5828 from entry #5826, p. 87.
[2]Mills, "according to several lexicons," p. 19.
[3]Mills, p. 20.
[4]Strong, "Hebrew," entry #6763, p. 100.
[5]Strong, "Hebrew," entry #6763, p. 100.

[6]Rodney Lloyd, teacher of Nov. 1980 class, Charismatic Perspective, at Rhema Bible Training Center.

Chapter 8
[1]Wilson, p. 197.
[2]Strong, "Hebrew," entry #1697.
[3]Wilson, p. 159.
[4]Theological Wordbook, entry #624, pp. 271, 272, and Strong, "Hebrew," entry #2428, p. 39.
[5]Strong, "Hebrew," entry #5850 from entry #5849, p. 87.
[6]*Webster's New Collegiate Dictionary,* s.v. "crown."

Chapter 9
[1]Strong, "Hebrew," entry #1692, p. 29.
[2]Dillow, p. 115.

Chapter 10
[1]Strong, "Greek," entry #435, p. 12, and entry #1135, p. 21.
[2]Theological Dictionary, p. 429.
[3]Strong, "Greek," entry #3616, p. 51.
[4]**Be subject to one another,** AMP. "Submission is a matter of attitude, while obedience is a matter of conduct," Nee, p. 107.
[5]Vine, s.v. "agree, agreement," Vol. I, p. 43.

Chapter 11
[1]Swindoll, p. 22.
[2]Swindoll, p. 22.
[3]Swindoll, p. 22.
[4]Strong, "Hebrew," entry #5288, p. 79.
[5]Swindoll, p. 23.

Chapter 12
[1]Wright, pp. 53, 198-200.
[2]Strong, "Hebrew," entry #3373, p. 52.

Chapter 13
[1]Swindoll, p. 37.
[2]Strong, "Hebrew," entry #7836, p. 114.

References

Brown, Francis. *The New Brown-Driver-Briggs-Gesenius Hebrew and English Lexicon*. Peabody: Hendrickson, © 1979 by Jay P. Green, Sr.

Dillow, Joseph C. *Solomon on Sex*. Nashville: Thomas Nelson, 1977.

Mills, Dick. *How To Have a Happy Marriage*. Tulsa: Harrison House, 1983.

Nee, Watchman. *Spiritual Authority*. New York: Christian Fellowship Publishers, Inc., 1972.

Strong, James. *Strong's Exhaustive Concordance of the Bible*. "Hebrew and Chaldee Dictionary," "Greek Dictionary of the New Testament." Nashville: Abingdon, 1890.

Swindoll, Charles R. *You and Your Child*. Nashville: Thomas Nelson, 1990.

Theological Wordbook of the Old Testament. Chicago: Moody Bible Institute, 1980.

Theological Dictionary of the New Testament. Grand Rapids: William B. Eerdmans, 1985.

Vine, W. E. *Expository Dictionary of New Testament Words*. Old Tappan: Fleming H. Revell, 1940.

Wilson, William. *Old Testament Word Studies*. Grand Rapids: Kregel, 1978.

Wright, Fred H. *Manners and Customs of Bible Lands*. Chicago: Moody Press, 1953.

Dr. Doyle "Buddy" Harrison

Ask **Buddy Harrison** who he is, and he will tell you, "I am a child of God, a son of God and an heir of God." Ask him what he does and he says, "I preach the Gospel — by sermon, book and tape." If he never preached another word, he knows he would still affect the world through prayer and the printed page. Because Buddy Harrison knows who he is in Christ and God's purpose for his life, he walks with assurance, ministers with a confidence and preaches with boldness and apostolic authority.

Numerous times in his life, Buddy has witnessed the miraculous, supernatural power of God. As a small boy, he was healed of polio. He has watched God heal, restore and deliver in his life and the lives of those he has ministered to. He and his wife Pat move in the gifts of the Spirit with a sensitivity and understanding.

More than 25 years ago, Buddy answered the call of God on his life and began his ministry in the ministry of helps as a music leader and youth minister. Today through the ministry of Faith Christian Fellowship International and the publishing company of Harrison House, Buddy is still in the ministry of helps. Both the ministry and the publishing company help men and women fulfill the call of God on their lives.

Buddy and Pat are known around the world for their anointed teachings from the Word of God and for their ability to communicate principles from the Word with a New Testament love. Because he purposes to obey God's Word and Spirit, Buddy has enjoyed tremendous success and favor.

To contact Buddy Harrison,
write:

Buddy Harrison
P. O. Box 35443
Tulsa, OK 74153

*Please include your prayer requests
and comments when you write.*

Other Books by Buddy Harrison

Four Keys To Power

How To Raise Your Kids in Troubled Times

Petitioning for the Impossible
The Prayer of Supplication

Understanding Authority for Effective Leadership

Getting in Position to Receive

Maintaining a Spirit-Filled Life

Just Do It

Count It All Joy
Eight Keys to Victory in
Times of Temptations, Test, and Trials
Coauthored by Van Gale

The Force of Mercy
The Gift Before and Beyond Faith
Coauthored by Michael Landsman

Available from your local bookstore.

HARRISON HOUSE
Tulsa, Oklahoma 74153

In Canada
books are available from:

Word Alive
P. O. Box 670
Niverville, Manitoba
CANADA R0A 1E0

The Harrison House Vision

Proclaiming the truth and the power
Of the Gospel of Jesus Christ
With excellence;

Challenging Christians to
Live victoriously,
Grow spiritually,
Know God intimately.